**THIRD
EDITION**

A NEW APPROACH
Christianity

A NEW APPROACH

THIRD EDITION

Christianity

Kevin O'Donnell

Hodder Murray

A MEMBER OF THE HODDER HEADLINE GROUP

The Publishers would like to thank the following for permission to reproduce copyright material:

Akg-images: pp 14, 16, 23, 26, 38, 45, 62 (right & left), 104; Akg-images/Cameraphoto: p 76; Akg-images/Erich Lessing: pp 9 (top), 24, 79, 141; Akg-images/Rabatti-Domingie: pp 21, 31; Alamy/Photofusion/Mo Wilson: p 120; Andes Press Agency: pp 49, 149 (bottom); AP Photo/Jacques Brinon: p 124 (left); AP Photo/Mark Humphrey: p 85; AP Photo/Plinio Lepri: p 74 (bottom); Photo/Silvia Izquierdo: p 56; AP Photo/Darko Vosinovich: p 78; British Library: p 134; Catholic Pictorial/Kim Till: p 99; Christian Aid/Adrian Arbib: p 127 (top right); Christian Aid/Max Hernandez: p 127 (top left); Christian Aid/Clive Shirley: p 127 (bottom); CIRCA: pp 23, 60, 100 (bottom), 103 (top right & bottom); CIRCA Photo Library/John Smith: p 110 (top right and top left); Corbis: pp 47, 49; Corbis/Archivo Iconografico, S.A.: p 145; Corbis/Arte & Immagini srl: p 59; Corbis/Dave Bartruff: p 90; Corbis/Bettman: pp 51, 67, 149 (top); Corbis/Philippe Eranian: p 124 (right); Corbis/Eve-Lotta Jansson: p 119; Corbis/Ed Kashi: p 114; Corbis/Earl & Nazima Kowall: p 65; Corbis/Michael S. Lewis: p 93; Corbis/Patsy Lynch: p 47; Corbis/Francis G. Mayer: p 69; Corbis/Reuters: p 64; Corbis/Reuters/Tony Gentile: p 74 (top); Corbis/Reuters/Reinhard Krause: p 148 (top); Corbis/Reuters/Faith Saribas: p 103; David Rose: pp 106, 107 (top), 108; Phil and Val Emmett: pp 84, 101 (top & bottom); Mary Evans Picture Library: p 80; PA Photos/EPA: p 81; PA Photos/Johnny Green: p 63; PA Photos/Maurice McDonald: p 143; Photodisk: pp 100 (top), 132, 148 (bottom); Rex Features/Action Press: p 107 (bottom); Rex Features/Ray Tang: p 33; Rylands Library, University of Manchester: p 135; © Tim Tiley Ltd: p 9 (bottom); Topham Picturepoint: pp 151, 152, 153; Topham/AP: pp 46, 83; WCC Publications for use of the WCC logo on p 82; World Religions Photo Library: pp 89, 110 (bottom), 117.

Scripture quotations taken from the HOLY BIBLE, NEW INTERNATIONAL VERSION.
Copyright © 1973, 1978, 1984 by International Bible Society.
Used by permission of Hodder & Stoughton Publishers,
A member of the Hodder Headline Group.
All rights reserved.
"NIV" is a registered trademark of International Bible Society.
UK trademark number 1448790.

Bible Societies/Collins for the extract from *Good News Bible* (1976); Church House Publishing for the extract from *Common Worship: Marriage Booklet* (2000); Hodder Christian Paperbacks for the extract from *When the Spirit Comes* by Colin Urquhart (1974); Papermac for the extract from *Jesus of Nazareth, King of the Jews* by Paula Fredriksen (2001); Penguin Books Ltd for the extract from *The Pilgrim's Progress* by John Bunyan (2005).

All artwork by Barking Dog Art.

Although every effort has been made to ensure that website addresses are correct at time of going to press, Hodder Murray cannot be held responsible for the content of any website mentioned in this book. It is sometimes possible to find a relocated web page by typing in the address of the home page for a website in the URL window of your browser.

Orders: please contact Bookpoint Ltd, 130 Milton Park, Abingdon, Oxon OX14 4SB. Telephone: (44) 01235 827720. Fax: (44) 01235 400454. Lines are open from 9.00–5.00, Monday to Saturday, with a 24-hour message answering service. Visit our website at www.hoddereducation.co.uk

© Kevin O'Donnell 2005
First published in 2005 by Hodder Murray, a member of the Hodder Headline Group
338 Euston Road
London NW1 3BH

Impression number   10 9 8 7 6 5 4 3
Year   2010 2009 2008 2007

Cover photo courtesy of Getty Images/Brand X Pictures/Steve Allen.
Typeset in Berling 10.5 by Fakenham Photosetting Limited, Fakenham, Norfolk.
Printed in Dubai.

A catalogue record for this title is available from the British Library.
ISBN : 978 0 340 81490 1

Contents

THE CREATOR

Christians believe that God is the creator of the universe, the ultimate source of all that is, and of all living things. There are different ideas about *how* he created – was it in six days or over thousands of years? However it happened, it has happened, and we are here, able to look up and around, wondering at the vastness of the cosmos and the complexity of nature.

Christians believe that human beings have been given a special role to look after our world as God's helpers, or as God's ambassadors. We have the power to protect nature or to harm it. Humans have the gift of free will, too. We can obey God or go our own way. We are not like robots.

JESUS

Christians believe that God stepped into his creation, rather like a novelist writing himself into his own story. He came in Jesus.

JEWISH HOPES

About 2000 years ago many of the Jewish people prayed for God to help them, to send a special man. Some hoped for a mighty warrior sent from God, a supernatural hero who would free the people from the Romans. Rome controlled the land of Judea and Galilee and its soldiers patrolled the villages and towns.

Others hoped for a holy man, a spiritual leader who would guide the people and bring peace and blessing to the world. Ancient prophecies spoke of a Messiah – a special, chosen man. He would be a new king who would bless and free his people.

JOHN THE BAPTIST

By the first century CE, some people were baptised in the River Jordan by a preacher called John. He had lived, praying and meditating, in the desert wilderness. He dressed in camel skins and ate locusts and wild honey. He was seen as a prophet, like one of the great prophets of old.

The people were baptised to prepare for the coming of God's special man. It was like turning over a new leaf. This offended some and gave great hope to others. The Coming One was

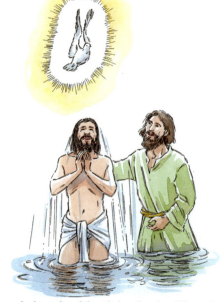

▲ Jesus is baptised by John in the River Jordan. Mark states that as he came out of the water he saw the spirit coming down on him like a dove (Mark 1:10–11).

known as 'the Messiah' in the Hebrew language, or, in the Greek language, 'the Christ'.

Jesus had a shattering experience of God as his Father when he was baptised by John. He believed that he was the Messiah.

Jesus had been a carpenter's son, Jesus son of Joseph (or, in the Jewish language, *Yeshua bar Yosif*). Now he was a man with a mission, and later, people called him 'Jesus Christ' (meaning 'Jesus the Messiah').

FATHER GOD

Jesus taught his disciples the 'Our Father' prayer.

> Our Father, who art in heaven, hallowed be thy name. Thy kingdom come; thy will be done. On earth as it is in heaven. For ever and ever. Amen.

God was close, like a loving father. The word he used was **Abba**. Jewish children used this of their fathers.

Jesus also taught that God's rule of peace and justice would dawn one day, and that we must forgive one another.

Jesus spoke to those on the fringes. He touched those no one else loved. His touch was said to heal.

▲ **Jesus helped those who were considered outcasts by society.**

THE CROSS

Jesus was rejected by the Roman and Jewish authorities. He was condemned to death on a cross. He was buried in a garden tomb and then, according to the Bible, he was raised up in a glorious new body, a spiritual body that can never die again. One day he will return to judge the world.

His followers believed he was raised from the dead and was still with them. They assembled together as a family to eat and drink holy communion – the meal Jesus had given them.

THE HOLY SPIRIT

The Holy Spirit is believed to be the invisible presence of God at work in people today. People can know peace with God and a have relationship with him.

One day, Christians believe, God will bring the world to an end and judge everything. We can enter into the glory of heaven, a life that is everlasting.

Christianity spread out from Jewish believers into the Roman Empire. Jesus had started a movement that called people together into a Gathering (or a 'Church' – that is what the word means). A new world faith began from the life and teachings of the humble, Spirit-filled man from Nazareth.

TEST YOURSELF

ABC

1 What do Christians believe about God coming to earth?
2 Who was John the Baptist?
3 What does 'Messiah' mean?
4 What would Jesus' actual name have been?
5 What does *Abba* mean?
6 What is taught about Father, Kingdom and Forgiveness in the Lord's Prayer?
7 Who is the Holy Spirit?

1

KEY WORDS

Abba – Aramaic word for 'Father'.
Adam – Hebrew word for a human being.
Creed – from Latin *credo*, 'I believe'. A list of beliefs.
Eternal – something that lasts forever.
Infinite – something that has no ending.
Ground of our Being – a term for God that tries to express his vastness, depth and mystery.
Holy Trinity – God as Father, Son and Holy Spirit.
Spirit – something invisible. In human terms, values and feelings. Of God, his invisible nature that can be everywhere at once.

KEY QUESTION
What is a Creed?

The key beliefs of the Christian faith are summarised in the Apostles' Creed. The Christian Church has drawn up lists of its important beliefs from time to time, and these are called **creeds**, from the Latin word *credo*, meaning 'I believe'. The Christian faith is believed: it cannot be proven like a mathematical equation. 'Faith' means trust. The Apostles' Creed was not actually written by the twelve apostles, but it was based on their teaching. It was certainly in existence by the fourth century CE:

> I believe in God, the Father almighty,
> Creator of heaven and earth.
> I believe in Jesus Christ, his only Son, our
> Lord.
> He was conceived by the power of the Holy
> Spirit
> And born of the Virgin Mary.
> He suffered under Pontius Pilate,
> Was crucified, died and was buried.
> He descended to the dead.
> On the third day he rose again.
> He ascended into heaven,
> And is seated at the right hand of the Father.
> He will come again to judge the living and
> The dead.
> I believe in the Holy Spirit,
> The holy catholic Church,

> The communion of saints,
> The forgiveness of sins,
> The resurrection of the body,
> And the life everlasting. Amen.

You will notice that God is spoken of in three ways, as Father, Son and Holy Spirit. This is known as the **Holy Trinity**. There are other creeds, too, such as the Nicene Creed that expanded the earlier Apostles' Creed in 325 CE.

KEY QUESTION
What do people mean by 'God'? Is this an old man in the sky?

GOD

Christians do not believe that God is an old man in the sky, like a very wise, cosmic Superman who lives on the right-hand side of the Milky Way. God is not a human being, but a force that is *everywhere* at once, invisible and eternal. Jesus said, 'God is Spirit'. **Spirit** is more like love, peace and freedom than like a man or woman. But God is more than these: Christians also believe that he can be prayed to and communicated with in a personal way, as two friends or two lovers would relate. So, God is like a force that is personal.

▲ **God is not really meant to be an old man in the sky.**

'FATHER'

St Paul says that Christians also have the right to address God in the same way that Jesus did, as *Abba*:

> For you did not receive a spirit that makes you a slave again to fear, but you received the Spirit of sonship. And by him we cry 'Abba, Father'. The Spirit himself testifies with our spirit that we are God's children.
>
> *Romans 8:15–16*

Is God a man, then? Calling God 'Father' does not mean that Christians think of him as literally male. God is Spirit, beyond this world. God is beyond masculine and feminine. Some people find it helpful to call God 'Mother', and God is compared with a caring mother in the Bible, at times, but Jesus used '*Abba*, Father', most of the time, and so modern believers do also. Some think this suggests authority and power as well as closeness.

▲ **This sculpture was influenced by the Isaiah passage, left.**

TASK BOX

Read through the following passage from the prophet Isaiah in the Hebrew Bible. What idea of God does this give?

Can a mother forget the baby
  at her breast
  and have no compassion on
  the child she has borne?
Though she may forget,
  I will not forget you!
See, I have engraved you on
  the palms of my hands ...
Isaiah 49:15–16a

KEY QUESTION

Do Christians have to believe that God made the world in six days, and that Adam and Eve were the first people?

Christians believe that God is the Creator. Only some believers think that God actually made the world in six days, and that the human race sprang from an actual couple, Adam and Eve. Other Christians take all this as symbolic poetry, an ancient attempt to say that the world came about because of God, and not just by chance. It might have taken millions of years for the universe to form, and God has been at work creating it all that time, and is still at work, for the universe is still changing and growing. Galaxies are expanding, and new forms of life are emerging.

Genesis

The biblical story of creation can be found in Genesis 1–2. There are slightly different accounts, here. These might have been two separate creation stories held by the Hebrews, which a later editor set out, side by side:

- Genesis 1–2:4 tells the story of the six-day creation, with God resting on the seventh day.
- Genesis 2:5–25 tells the story of the creation of Adam, the animals and then Eve.

These are not easy to harmonise, for in the first, animals come first and then humans. In the second, a man is made, then animals, and then a woman. They both have their meanings and their message. If these are symbolic truth and not literal truth, then they can still have much to say to people today.

The six days can be taken as a poetic idea. These are then six stages of creation. Perhaps each one took thousands of years in fact. When read like this, the first chapter of Genesis fits almost exactly into modern scientific ideas (water, simple life forms, life on the land and in the air, animals and humans).

Genesis 2 can be read as a parable about the first people. **Adam** means 'human' in Hebrew; Adam is then 'Everyman', each one of us. Some think that God did start to work specifically on two primitive people, an actual Adam and Eve. Perhaps God could have taken early ape-men and given them his Spirit and a rational mind. Others see our emergence as spiritual, rational beings as a gradual process, slowly coming about after thousands of years of evolution.

How and why

It is often said that science deals with the 'how' questions and religion with the 'why'. Science deals with mechanics: how things work and link together. Religion looks at the bigger picture and asks a different sort of question: 'What is the point of it all?' For example, biology tells us that human beings are on earth to reproduce the species. People wonder if that is the only reason.

TASK BOX

A Parable

There was once a man who built a factory. It was a factory that made the parts to build another factory. On and on he went, until he had a long series of factories making the parts to make yet more factories. One day, someone asked him why he was bothering to do this. Surely, there was no point to all his work unless we needed the factories for something else, too?

Life is like that. If human beings are just here to reproduce, then why? There must be more to it than that.

How does this parable relate to the question of creation and the issue of 'how' and 'why'?

A believer would say that we are here to worship God and to love one another, as well.

Persons and forces

Science tries to sum the universe up by mathematics, forces and chemicals. These things are all true, but perhaps there is another point of view to be considered, too. We, as people, cannot just be reduced to these mechanical forces. We are thinking, feeling beings. Perhaps we need personal values and explanations of the universe, too, and that is where belief in God comes in. Scientists might be able to explain how everything came to be, linking everything up through causes and effects back to the Big Bang, but they have told us nothing about its purpose.

Big mystery

God, for Christians, is beyond human understanding, and is a mystery. Christians do not think that God is one object among all the others in the universe – even a superior one. God is different, and contains all the universe within himself. He is not just one lump or shape of some kind in one corner of the galaxy, but present in all things. God is therefore of a different order of being. The theologian Paul Tillich coined the term 'the **Ground of our Being**', to suggest that God is not floating about 'up there' somewhere, but is to be found deep within people, as the source of our life and very being. God is deep at the centre of all things, flowing through everything.

Think of a sponge that is pushed into a river. The water soaks all the way through it and flows around it.

God is like the water, and the universe is like the sponge.

Explain why this is so.

TEST YOURSELF

1 What is the difference between a literal and a symbolic understanding of Genesis 1 and 2?
2 What might Adam and Eve stand for?
3 What is the difference between the questions 'how' and 'why'?

Because he [God] may well be loved, but not thought. By love he can be caught and held, but by thinking never.

The Cloud of Unknowing

KEY QUESTION

'Who made God?' – and is that possible?

God is meant to be **infinite** (without limit) and **eternal** (without beginning or end). Humans are both finite and temporal. This means that we have limits and have a start and a finish (we are born, and we die). Nothing we know lasts forever. Everything starts and finishes. We have symbols of eternity, such as a circle, or infinite numbers like π that just keep going on and on (3.14159 ...), but nothing out there actually lasts forever. That makes it difficult to imagine that God just is; God is said to have no start or finish. God makes things, but nothing made God. (If anything did, it would be greater than God – which is impossible.)

God has to be a mystery, for finite and temporal beings can never fully understand the infinite and the eternal. Some think of God as a vast, mighty ocean, and humans are on the shore, splashing about, but beyond is darkness and mystery.

TASK BOX

What ideas about the nature of God are found in these two simple stories?

- A little fish once went on a quest for a thing called the sea. He went all over looking for it. A wiser, older fish said, 'It's all around you and within you. It's been here all the time. You live in it!'

- Two friends walked along the seashore. They saw a little boy running to and fro with a bucket. He was constantly filling a hole with sea water. The little boy looked at them and said, 'I'm trying to fit the sea into my hole!' They both laughed.

▲ A vast, raging sea is a fitting symbol for God, to some people. There seems to be no limit, no start or finish.

A New Approach – Christianity

Can the Existence of God be Proved?

Believers feel this is a matter of faith, of trust, but some have attempted to prove there must be a God. Their theories are given special notes:

1 The Ontological Argument (from Greek _ontos_: 'being')

St Anselm said that God is the Supreme Being. If our minds can think of such a Being, then he must exist. If God is just an idea, then God cannot be the Supreme Being, for to be such a Being, God must exist in reality and not just in the mind. Sceptics say this means that anything we can imagine, like the moon being made of green cheese, must exist. It is nonsense and a circular argument. Anselm meant, though, that we would have no idea of, or no feeling for God, if God did not exist. Why is the idea in our minds? What put it there if it is all make believe?

2 The Cosmological Argument (from Greek _cosmos_: 'world')

St Thomas Aquinas argued that every effect has a cause; therefore the universe needs a First Cause. Others reply, 'Why can't the universe just have happened or always have existed?'

3 The Teleological Argument (from Greek _telos_: 'purpose')

Aquinas also pointed out that there is a harmony and a design in the universe. This must mean that it is here for a purpose and has a Creator. Some would reply that this harmony just happened by chance, maybe against astronomical odds, but it could just have happened.

4 The Moral Argument

In the 18th century, Immanuel Kant argued that our consciences knew, instinctively, what was right and wrong. He felt that this knowledge, placed in our souls, must have come from a good God, behind all things.

Can you think of any other 'proofs' of God's existence? Write these out. Are all the 'proofs' certain, or are other interpretations possible?

TASK BOX

In the 'hot seat'!

Get into a group, with a circle of chairs and one empty chair. Prepare some ideas in your group about why God might or might not exist. Each member has to take a turn to sit in the 'hot seat' (the empty chair) and present a point of view. The others of you can then question the person in the hot seat.
For example:
'Hot Seat': The world must have come from somewhere.
Question: But might it have all been by chance?

THE HOLY TRINITY

KEY QUESTION

What does it mean to call God 'Father, Son and Holy Spirit'? Are these three gods?

▲ Rublev's Trinity – one artist's idea of the Trinity, imagined as three angels around a table.

Speaking of God as 'the Ground of our Being' sounds impersonal and makes God seem remote. Yet Christians believe that God is involved in the world, and in a personal way with individuals. They speak of God as 'Father, Son and Holy Spirit'. This is the Trinity (from *tri-unity*, 'three-in-one'). To imagine how three things can be one, Christians suggest thinking of a triangle, with three sides or angles but one shape. This is only helpful up to a point, though, for such things are abstract and impersonal, whereas God can be related to.

Also, the three sections of the Trinity do different things, though they all work together. Language about the Trinity stretches our imaginations and our understanding, for the Trinity is not meant to be an organising committee of three, but one thing with three aspects or relationships within it:

- The Father is the Creator.
- The Son is the Saviour or Redeemer.
- The Spirit is the one who gives new life and makes holy (the Sanctifier).

The Father is the Creator, the Son is the Redeemer, and the Spirit is the Life-giver, or Sanctifier (one who makes holy). These are not taken to be three gods, but one God working in three ways.

This threefold pattern to God's activity can be seen in various New Testament writings, such as a prayer of St Paul, known as 'the Grace': 'The grace of our Lord Jesus Christ, the love of God, and the fellowship of the Holy Spirit, be with us all, ever more' (2 Corinthians 13:14).

TASK BOX

In the story of the baptism of Jesus, a threefold pattern can be seen, too. See if you can spot the presence of Father, Son and Spirit at work in the following passage from Mark:

As Jesus was coming up out of the water, he saw heaven being torn open and the Spirit descending on him like a dove. And a voice came from heaven: 'You are my Son, whom I love; with you I am well pleased.'
Mark 1:10–11

When the creeds were being written, people began to talk about the three *persons* in God – of Father, Son and Holy Spirit. They did not mean three individual *minds*, or *spirits*, which all love each other perfectly. The *persons* are all part of *one* thing: three relations within God.

Some interpret the 'persons' in God as roles or aspects. There is a danger here that people will think that Father, Son and Holy Spirit are only three temporary ways of God being God. Each role, or person, is then seen like an actor's mask that he wears and discards: he wears the Father's mask to create the world, the Son's mask to save it, and the Spirit's mask to work in people.

CREATOR REDEEMER SANCITIFIER

▲ **Christians do not believe that God ever stops being three-things-in-one. He doesn't take one mask off and put on another.**

The Church teaches that the three ways of being God – call them roles or persons – are eternal. God is threefold in himself, and not only in the world as people experience him. God's threefoldness suggests that God is dynamic, able to relate to himself and to act outwards into the world. Yet, this is a mystery beyond our understanding: three in one; one in three.

1 Describe the meaning of the word faith. [2]
2 Explain the reasons that people might have for believing in God. [6]
3 How do Christians explain the Holy Trinity? [8]
4 'The world could not exist if it had not been created.'
   Do you agree? Give reasons for your opinion, showing you have understood other points of view. Make sure you refer to Christian beliefs. [4]
5 What is meant by the Trinity? [2]
6 Describe what it means to say God is transcendent. [3]
7 Explain how the Apostles' Creed shows a belief in the Trinity. [4]
8 Give three reasons a Christian might have for believing in God. [6]

Assignment

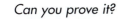

Some lively and visual websites exploring the idea of God are as follows:

Can you prove it?
🕷 www.request.org.uk/issues/ evidence/evidence01.htm

Finding God –
🕷 www.arimathea.co.uk/ finding.htm

WEBLINKS

REMEMBER

▶ God is understood as an invisible Spirit and not as a cosmic Superman.
▶ God is mysterious and mighty to believers, but can also be close and prayed to.
▶ God can still be behind the processes of evolution and the Big Bang.
▶ God acts in the world in three ways: as Father, Son and Holy Spirit. God is always these three things in himself, to a believer.

2

KEY WORDS

Ascension – Jesus' return to heaven.

Atonement – making peace, making up for doing something wrong.

Christ – the Greek word for Messiah, or Anointed One.

Demi-gods – half-human, half-god figures in Greek and Roman myths.

God the Son – the Second Person of the Trinity.

Incarnation – the idea that God became a human being in Jesus.

Paraclete – a helper, counsellor or advocate; a name for the Holy Spirit.

Parousia – the return of Christ at the end of time.

Son of God – a term with many meanings, such as 'holy person', the King, or, of Jesus, the Second Person of the Trinity.

Word – part of God acting in the world.

KEY QUESTION

Do Christians believe that Jesus was literally God's son?

THE SON OF GOD

▲ A Byzantine icon painting – *The Madonna*.
The Virgin Mary with the child Jesus.

The Apostles' Creed begins by calling Jesus God's only Son. This is a common and often misunderstood title that Christians use for Jesus.

It sounds as though Christians believe that Jesus is the physical offspring of God, just as a person has an earthly father. It can even make Mary sound like God's wife! Christianity is not really the story of 'God and son', but of part of God at work supremely in a human life.

In the East, the phrase 'son of' is used in a variety of ways. It can mean somebody's actual son, but it can also be used in a symbolic way – to say that someone is like someone else. So, 'son of a camel' is an insult that suggests that someone is very rude and ill-mannered. To call someone a 'son of God' means that they are very holy and God-like.

The title '**Son of God**' is poetic. It is a metaphor: it stands for something that should not be taken word for word. To call someone *the* Son of God means that he is the holiest person ever to have lived, the person who shows what God is like more than anyone else. Jesus was therefore to the early Christians a man full of God (though the title came to mean much more later on).

The background

At the time of Jesus, outstanding people were called 'son of God' by the Romans. This title meant the person was extra special, but the more uneducated probably thought the person's father had actually been a god. The Greek and Roman myths had many stories of gods mating with human women and producing **demi-gods** (half god; half human) like Heracles. Some Christian converts might have understood the story of the virgin birth in this way: that Jesus was a demi-god or that he had been the heavenly Son of God who had come down to save people. Yet, the Church taught that it was God who had come down, and not a lesser being.

To find out all the things 'Son of God' means to Christians, it is useful to start with the Old Testament, which was the only Bible the first Christians had before the New Testament was written. Here, we find that faithful Jews are sometimes called 'son of God', and the whole people of Israel were called 'sons of God' (as in Hosea 11:1, where God says, 'When Israel was a child, I loved him, / and out of Egypt I called my son').

The Kings of Israel were called 'son of God', too:

> I will proclaim the decree of the Lord:
>
> He said to me, 'You are my Son;
>   today I have become your Father.'
> *Psalm 2:7*

The King was the special servant of God, who was supposed to rule the people with justice and set an example for the people to follow. 'Son of God' was a metaphor, therefore, for a faithful, holy servant of God; it suggested that the person was very close to God.

The first Christians used the title 'Son of God' against this background. It originally meant the Jewish Messiah, the King of the Jews, the special Servant of God. 'Christ' was the Greek translation of the Hebrew title 'Messiah.' It was not Jesus' surname. It could also mean a very holy man. To them, Jesus was a man full of God, through whom salvation was going to come to the world. It was only later that the title suggested that Jesus was divine, and more than an ordinary human. It was the belief in the resurrection that started the Church thinking that Jesus was *uniquely* one with God. When they thought of Jesus, they thought of God and man, together. The two were inseparable.

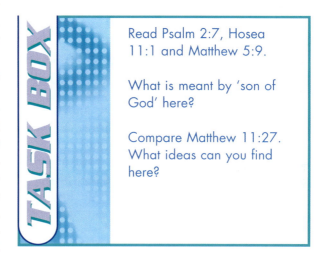

TASK BOX

Read Psalm 2:7, Hosea 11:1 and Matthew 5:9.

What is meant by 'son of God' here?

Compare Matthew 11:27. What ideas can you find here?

KEY QUESTION
Was Jesus human or divine?

THE INCARNATION

The word **incarnation** means 'in the body'. Christians came to believe that Jesus was not just a good man, nor just the holiest prophet that has ever lived. They believe that God and man were joined together in his life and that Jesus was, in some way, God become man.

This does not mean that Christians think that Jesus was like a puppet controlled by God, or that God disguised himself in a human body, as though he were putting on a suit of clothes. Jesus was not a mask, a secret identity for God, like Clark Kent is for Superman: Jesus was a real human being with his own feelings and his own mind. Yet, he was linked, uniquely, to the being of God.

God came down to earth in Jesus

Christians today take this as symbolic language, meaning that the presence of God was focused in the life of Jesus more than anywhere else on earth; God is supposed to be everywhere and in all things, but some things are vehicles for his presence more than others. The Church teaches that there was a deliberate and unique joining of God with the human being, Jesus, from the moment of conception in Mary's womb, so that the life of Jesus is a unique act of God in human history.

The manner and nature of the joining of God and man in Jesus is seen as a mystery that ultimately defies words. For the creeds, it was important to say that it was God, and not an angel or his deputy, that was in Jesus, and also that Jesus was a full human being, and not some strange Superman figure. The Gospels, for example, are clear that Jesus could feel pain like the rest of us. Jesus was not a pagan demi-god pretending to be a man, but something different: God incarnate.

 For Christians, as a human being, Jesus shows us what we are; as God, Jesus shows us what God is like.

The developing message

The belief in the incarnation developed gradually, but was there very early on in Christian history. Peter's message, soon after the resurrection, was that Jesus was a man blessed by God, as shown by the signs and wonders God had worked through Jesus.

Mark's Gospel, the earliest of the four, presents Jesus as the Messiah whose words have a striking authority and whose miracles are seen as the first signs of the Kingdom breaking through. Jesus is a man full of the Spirit who has an unnerving effect on those around him. This is how people react when he preaches:

'The people were all so amazed that they asked each other, "What is this? A new teaching – and with authority!" ' (Mark 1:27).

The Gospels of Matthew and Luke, some 15 to 20 years later, present essentially the same picture. God had acted in a striking and unique way in his envoy, Jesus of Nazareth. Jesus possessed a unique authority and a special relationship with God as Father.

In John's Gospel, by the end of the first century CE, Jesus is seen as the **Word** of God incarnate, God manifest in flesh.

The 'Word of God' is a metaphor for God acting in the world. The Gospel closes with the confession of Thomas when he encounters the risen Christ: 'My Lord and my God!' (John 20:28). Yet, much earlier passages than John, in the writings of St Paul, had expressed similar ideas: Jesus was to be worshipped as God (compare, e.g., Philippians 2:5–11).

> ... that at the name of Jesus every knee should bow,
> in heaven and on earth and under the earth,
> and every tongue confess that Jesus Christ is Lord,
> to the glory of God the Father.
>
> *Philippians 2:10–11*

Read the following passages. How has belief in Jesus developed between these two statements?

Men of Israel, listen to this: Jesus of Nazareth was a man accredited by God to you by miracles, wonders and signs, which God did among you through him, as you yourselves know.
Acts 2:22

The Word became flesh and made his dwelling among us. We have seen his glory, the glory of the One and Only, who came from the Father, full of grace and truth.
John 1:14

REMEMBER

- The Synoptic Gospels – Matthew, Mark and Luke – have a more primitive view of Jesus. He is filled with God and has a special authority and relationship with God.
- John has a more developed theology – Jesus is the Word of God made flesh.
- St Paul, writing even earlier than the finished Synoptic Gospels, speaks of Jesus in divine, exalted terms. Thus, Christians began thinking about Jesus in this way very early on.

'SON OF GOD' AND 'GOD THE SON'

The Nicene Creed

We believe in one God, the Father, the Almighty, maker of heaven and earth, of all that is, seen and unseen.

We believe in one Lord, Jesus **Christ**, the only Son of God, eternally begotten of the Father, God from God, Light from Light, true God from true God, begotten, not made, of one Being with the Father; through him all things were made. For us and for our salvation he came down from heaven, was incarnate from the Holy Spirit and the Virgin Mary and was made man. For our sake he was crucified under Pontius Pilate; he suffered death and was buried. On the third day he rose again in accordance with the Scriptures; he ascended into heaven and is seated at the right hand of the Father. He will come again in glory to judge the living and the dead, and his kingdom will have no end.

We believe in the Holy Spirit, the Lord, the giver of life, who proceeds from the Father and the Son, who with the Father and the Son is worshipped and glorified, who has spoken through the prophets. We believe in one holy catholic and apostolic Church. We acknowledge one baptism for the forgiveness of sins. We look for the resurrection of the dead, and the life of the world to come. Amen.

The Nicene Creed speaks of the Son as being 'God from God, Light from Light'. This does not mean the human being, Jesus of Nazareth, but the God who was present, or incarnate in him. The Creed was written to point out that it was wrong to teach that a lesser god was in Jesus than the true God. **God the Son**, then, equals the part of God that was in Jesus, united to him. Christians often confuse 'Son of God' with 'God the Son', but they were originally different. 'Son of God' originally meant the man full of God; 'God the Son' means the God who filled the man. (Christians see these as two sides of the same coin: there is one person who is human and God.)

People might debate which parts of the Gospels are literally true, historically accurate or symbolic stories. They are all about Jesus, a real man who had a lasting impact. He still inspires people today. Read the following quotation. Might this help people believe there was something divine about Jesus, also?

Jesus means something to our world because a mighty spiritual force streams forth from Him and flows through our time also. This fact can neither be shaken nor confirmed by any historical discovery. It is the solid foundation of Christianity.

Albert Schweitzer, **The Quest of the Historical Jesus**

▲ **Jesus was not a Superman figure, but real flesh and blood, and he could feel pain.**

When reading the Gospels, we are faced with a Teacher who challenges us. There is something mysterious about him for believers, a quality that calls them to follow. Read through these thoughts from the German Christian philosopher Albert Schweitzer (1875–1965):

He comes to us as One unknown, without a name, as of old, by the lake-side, he came to those men who knew Him not. He speaks to us the same word, 'Follow thou me!' And sets us to the tasks He has to fulfil in our own time. He commands. And to those who obey Him, whether they be wise or simple, he will reveal Himself ...

THE CROSS

> ### KEY QUESTION
> Why do Christians believe that Jesus' death on the cross saved humanity?

The cross is the most important Christian symbol. The story of the crucifixion of Jesus stands, with that of his resurrection, at the centre of the Christian faith. Christians understand the story of the cross in various ways. There is no one way of seeing it, but all say that God was doing something in Jesus on the cross.

 God was reconciling the world to himself in Christ ...

2 Corinthians 5:19

▲ A crucifix, dated c. 1240.

These are modern ways of understanding the story of the cross. The following are some much older ones that sound strange to modern ears at first. They still contain much insight and wisdom, and inspire modern believers just as they did centuries ago.

A sacrifice for sin

An early way of understanding the death of Jesus was as a sacrifice. The Jews had various sacrifices, such as the **atonement** sacrifice. This one is particularly relevant to the story of Jesus. Atonement means to make up for something. The blood of various animals was sprinkled on the Temple altar and was thought to purify people from sin. This sounds strange to us, but people in ancient times thought that an animal's blood offered to God could pay the price for human sins. Jesus had died and shed his blood. The blood of the Son of God was more powerful, and could purify the whole human race. It was the best sacrifice that could ever be offered, and so the Christians stopped offering atonement sacrifices.

Here are some ways that modern Christians have of understanding the cross:

- God came in Jesus but God would not force anyone to listen, and he gave them the freedom to reject him. They did reject him and nailed him to a cross. The cross shows people, today, that God is love, and that he will forgive people if they will turn to him, no matter what they have done. Looking at the cross should make people sorry for their sins.
- The cross shows that God can suffer; he is not a million miles away in heaven. God is involved in the struggles of everyday life. God stands alongside people who suffer and gives them courage.
- The cross shows that God has entered all the darkness in the world. He has gone through death, and come out the other side. He has shown that the darkness can be transformed, and that good is stronger than evil in the end.

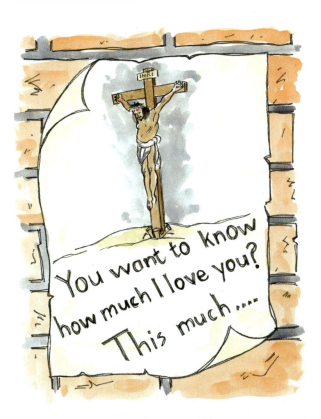

You want to know how much I love you? This much....

A victory over evil

The cross probably sounds more like a victory of evil over good. However, the early Church teachers argued that Jesus had defeated the devil by dying on the cross. They said this was because Jesus had shed his blood to purify the human race. The devil thought he had destroyed the Son of God, only to have his plan backfire.

The resurrection showed the victory of Jesus over death and the devil. This view might sound a little strange today, but good is seen to triumph over evil as Jesus rose; light overcame darkness; hope came out of despair. That is something that all believers can affirm in this day and age.

▲ Jesus is sometimes pictured as the Lamb of God, a reference to the sacrifices in the Temple.

The justice of God is satisfied

Another way of understanding the cross was to use the language of the law courts. People have sinned; therefore they stand guilty before God. God is their judge. God is holy and demands justice, but he is also love, and so he became man and took the punishment for sin Himself. It is like a judge passing sentence and then standing in the dock to take the punishment, or demanding a fine and then writing the cheque herself.

THE RESURRECTION

> ### KEY QUESTION
> What do Christians mean when they say that 'Jesus lives'?

The resurrection is mentioned in nearly every book of the New Testament. It is the central belief of Christianity. Indeed, the whole of Christian theology – all its reflection on God and Christ – comes from that belief.

The disciples were frightened and ran for their lives when Jesus was crucified, and yet something made them regroup in Jerusalem and boldly go out preaching their message.

The New Testament letters do not describe the resurrection in any detail. They refer to it as the victory of Jesus over death, and also as the new life Christians felt inside. It is something that happened to Jesus, and something that can happen in the believer: 'And if the Spirit of him who raised Jesus from the dead is living in you, he who raised Christ from the dead will also give life to your mortal bodies through his Spirit, who lives in you' (Romans 8:11).

More information is given in 1 Corinthians 15, where Paul describes the appearances of the risen Christ to the Twelve and other disciples. Paul describes the resurrection life as being in a spiritual body, the nature of which is beyond human understanding: when the body is buried, it is mortal; when raised, it will be immortal. This great hope began with what happened to Jesus after his death.

The resurrection is seen as a triumph, a transformation and as a future hope.

- *A triumph* – the resurrection is seen as God's blessing on all Jesus said and did, when, in the eyes of many, he was a failure for having been crucified.
- *A transformation* – the resurrection is not simply about a dead man coming back to life, but a transformation. Jesus lives *in God* as a spiritual, glorified being.
- *A future hope* – the resurrection is seen as a pledge that all the darkness in life will one day be turned into glorious light. All that has happened in the universe will not just fade away and be lost: it has a fulfilment to come in God.

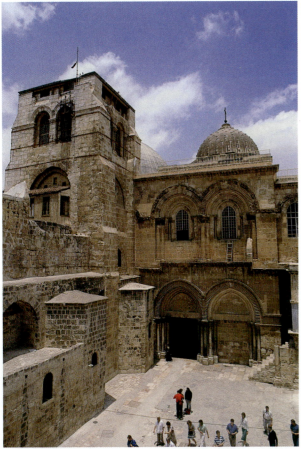

▲ **The Church of the Holy Sepulchre in Jerusalem, where Jesus is said to have been buried and raised up.**

> I consider that our present sufferings are not worth comparing with the glory that will be revealed in us.
>
> *Romans 8:18*

▲ The Resurrection by Matthias Grunewald. The artist tried to give a sense of majesty, mystery and power in the blazing light coming from Jesus. Jesus is something beyond the physical.

DID JESUS RISE FROM THE DEAD?

> ### KEY QUESTION
> Can the resurrection be explained away?

The story of the resurrection sounds almost unbelievable. Many have tried to argue that it is based upon misunderstandings.

Someone stole the body

If the disciples had tricked people in this way, it is hard to see how they would have been prepared to die for their faith. The Gospels also tell us that the tomb was heavily guarded by Roman soldiers. The story of the empty tomb alone did not produce faith in the resurrection, though: the appearances did this as well, and the feeling of new life inside. Some Christians don't believe in the empty tomb story: they think Jesus rose only spiritually.

The women went to the wrong tomb

Some suggest that the women went to the wrong tomb by mistake. They were mourning and upset and could easily have become confused. There were many such tombs cut into the rock. Remember all that has been said about appearances and inner feelings above, though, and note that the disciples did not trust the women's story at first. The disciples went to look for themselves and found the tomb empty.

Jesus didn't really die

He did die sooner than expected (in six hours; crucifixion victims could linger on for a day or two). But this could be explained by the fact that he was whipped before being crucified. Some people died from the whipping alone, and people did not usually have both punishments together. If Jesus had recovered in the tomb, he would have been a physical mess, and would not have been able to move the huge tombstone, or convince anyone that he had risen in glory! John's Gospel tells us that a Roman soldier thrust a spear into Jesus' side and blood and water poured out. This was a sure sign that he had died of suffocation (John19:34).

The disciples felt guilty

The disciples' sense of guilt when they deserted Jesus or their sorrow at losing him might explain the sightings of Jesus (as some people claim to 'see' dead relatives because they are so sorry to lose them). However, it cannot really explain the sense of new life and courage that the disciples and the early Christians who joined the Church later on felt. Guilty people do not make other people feel free, but guilty too. The disciples seemed to have been surprised, too. They were not expecting Jesus to rise. They had run away, were in hiding and were scared. Some of the Gospel accounts suggest that Jesus was very real – he could eat fish with them (Luke 24:42–3). He was no hallucination. Paul says in 1 Corinthians 15:6 that once over 500 people saw him together.

Dead people don't rise

There is no scientific proof of life after death, and the bodies of people just lie in the graves and rot. This does not mean that people cannot live on spiritually in some new form in another world or on another level of reality. This would be beyond investigation by science, though you get occasional stories of ghosts, visions and near-death experiences. Science cannot prove it or disprove it: it is a question of faith. The disappearance of Jesus' body is seen as a 'one off' by Christians, because he was so special as the Son of God. His flesh was not left to rot.

Jesus lives on in his teaching

Jesus thus lives on, in a manner of speaking, in his teachings about love, peace and forgiveness, rather as Elvis is said to live on through his music. Yet that is not the teaching of the New Testament. It teaches that Jesus of Nazareth somehow *survived death* and promised his followers the same could happen to them.

TASK BOX

a   What are the strengths and weaknesses of the above arguments?
b   What arguments would Christians offer to try to prove the resurrection?
c   Work out a role play where a few people argue with a priest or minister. They say that God is distant, does not care or should get more involved. The priest tries to tell them about the incarnation, about Jesus on the cross and what this shows us about God for Christians.
d   Another group can perform a different role play. A few of you pretend to confess to a Catholic priest. Act as if you don't care about the proper meaning of confession, and are playing it just for laughs. He takes you and shows you a large crucifix. He asks you if you still don't care. What might you say then?

THE ASCENSION

▲ A 15th century Russian icon showing the ascension of Christ, with his disciples below.

The writer of the Acts of the Apostles includes a short story describing how the risen Christ left his disciples by rising into the air, known as the **ascension**: 'After he said this, he was taken up before their very eyes, and a cloud hid him from their sight' (Acts 1:9).

The New Testament letters speak of Jesus being raised up and exalted. St Paul, for example, quotes from an early Christian hymn:

> And being found in appearance as a man,
>   he humbled himself
>   and became obedient to death – even to
>   death on a cross!
> Therefore God has exalted him to the
>   highest place
>   and gave him the name that is above
>   every name ...
> *Philippians 2:8–9*

The popular idea of the shape of the world in the past was that the earth was at the centre, with heaven up above, hell below, and the stars and planets moving around the dome of the sky in their various orbits. Many of the early Christians would have pictured Jesus going back to God in the way Acts describes it: he would go up to heaven above. To us, this is ridiculous, for there is nothing but miles and miles of empty space above the earth.

The idea of Jesus ascending on high and sitting at the right-hand side of God is powerful picture-language, however. The writer of Acts probably understood the ascension story as a symbol, for he was an educated man and would have known more about the nature of the world than many.

The idea of going up on high suggests power and success. The athlete who wins a gold medal stands above the others on the podium. The best-selling record is called the 'top of the pops'. To say that Jesus ascended is to say that Jesus had become the most important person in human history; that he now lives in God and has a cosmic significance. It means that Jesus reigns over all the forces in the world, that good has won over evil.

TEST YOURSELF

1 How did many ancient people understand the world?
2 What did the image of being on the right-hand side of the Father suggest?
3 What do symbols of height suggest?

THE PAROUSIA (THE SECOND COMING)

Christians believe that Jesus is reigning over the earth, but that the Kingdom has not yet fully come. Many people suffer, and evil is still at work. Christians think that Christ will return in some way: he has not yet finished with the world. The special word for the return of Christ is the **parousia**. This is a Greek word meaning 'the presence', and was used of kings and rulers returning to their court. This area of Christian belief is called **eschatology**, which means the study of the last things, or the end of time.

Read the following passages about the return of Christ. List the events that occurred and the feelings aroused by them:

But in those days, following that distress,
'the sun will be darkened,
   and the moon will not give its light;
the stars will fall from the sky,
   and the heavenly bodies will be shaken.'
At that time men will see the Son of Man coming in clouds with great power and glory. And he will send his angels and gather his elect from the four winds, from the ends of the earth to the ends of the heavens.
Mark 13:24–7

I saw heaven standing open and there before me was a white horse, whose rider is called Faithful and True. With justice he judges and makes war. His eyes are like blazing fire, and on his head are many crowns. He has a name written on him that no-one knows but he himself. He is dressed in a robe dipped in blood, and his name is the Word of God. ... Out of his mouth comes a sharp sword with which to strike down the nations. ... On his robe, and on his thigh he has this name written: king of kings and lord of lords.
Revelation 19:11–13, 15, 16

Various New Testament passages describe the parousia in vivid, striking poetry. Very few Christians take all this word for word. It is obviously poetry, full of symbols and hidden meanings. Many Christians do think that Jesus will actually return in some way, however, and that everyone will see him. He will come again in glory; he will not be reborn as an ordinary person.

Other Christians find this hard to believe. Instead, they think Christ will return as a spiritual force that will cover the earth.

The vivid poetry that the parousia hope is expressed in is a style called apocalyptic (which means 'revealing hidden things'). It was popular amongst the Jews at the time of Jesus. It developed from the book of Daniel onwards, and one passage in that book lies behind most of the imagery in the parousia idea, a vision of a human being (or a 'son of man') placed upon a throne by God: 'In my vision at night I looked, and there before me was one like a son of man, coming with the clouds of heaven. He approached the Ancient of Days and was led into his presence. He was given authority, glory and sovereign power; all peoples, nations, and men of every language worshipped him' (Daniel 7:13–14).

TEST YOURSELF

1 What different interpretations of the return of Christ are there?
2 What does Daniel 7:13–14 say?

THE HOLY SPIRIT

KEY QUESTION
Who is the Holy Spirit?

The Apostles' Creed states, 'I believe in the Holy Spirit'. The Holy Spirit is mentioned throughout the Bible. In Genesis, at the creation of the world, the Spirit hovered over the chaos, bringing life and order (Genesis 1:2). The Spirit breathed into Adam, making him a living being (Genesis 2:7). The Spirit was sent on the many

Old Testament prophets to give the gift of prophecy (Ezekiel 2:1–2), and the Spirit constantly brings life to the earth (Psalm 104:30).

> When you send your Spirit,
>   they are created,
> and you renew the face of the earth.
>
> *Psalm 104:30*

The Spirit, like the Word, is the creative presence and power of God in the world. In the Hebrew Bible, God sends his Spirit and his Word to do his work. In the New Testament, the Spirit and the Word are revealed as part of the Trinity, alongside the Father.

Jesus promised to send the Holy Spirit after he left the earth.

Literally it means 'one who comes alongside someone else'.

The Spirit is symbolised by various things:

> And I will ask the Father, and he will give you another Counsellor to be with you forever – the Spirit of truth.
>
> *John 14:16–17a*

- *Wind* – the Spirit is an invisible force.
- *Oil* – the Spirit soothes and brings healing.
- *Dove* – the Spirit brings peace from above.
- *Fire* – the Spirit is a holy power.

The Spirit brings new life to Christians and inspires them to follow Jesus and to understand his teaching. The Holy Spirit is God's presence in the world, and in the believer.

▲ The paraclete is a helper, one who comes to our aid, who stands up for us, puts an arm around our shoulders and so on.

In John 14–16, Jesus speaks of the Spirit as the **Paraclete** (a Greek word) he would send in his place on earth. A paraclete is a 'helper', 'comforter', or even 'counsel for the defence'.

TASK BOX

Look up these passages and see which symbol is used of the Spirit: Acts 2:1–4; John 3:8; Matthew 3:16.

TEST YOURSELF

1 What does the Spirit do at creation?
2 What did the Spirit do for Adam?
3 What did the Spirit do for the prophets?
4 What does the Spirit do for all living things?
5 What did Jesus promise to send?

1 Describe the meaning of the word Christ. [2]
2 Explain what Christians believe about the incarnation. [6]
3 Explain the symbolism Christians use to represent the Holy Spirit. [8]
4 'Christian beliefs are unbelievable.'
Do you agree? Give reasons for your opinion, showing that you have considered other points of view. [4]
5 What is meant by the Paraclete? [5]
6 Describe four symbols used in Christianity for the Holy Spirit. [8]
7 'People can't believe in a presence they can't see.'
What would Christians say about this? Bring in some ideas about the Holy Spirit. [7]

REMEMBER

- Jesus is seen as the unique incarnation of God.
- The cross was seen as redemptive, bringing the forgiveness of God.
- Jesus' resurrection involved the 'empty tomb' story, appearances and a feeling of new life within the disciples.
- The Ascension is about the power and significance Christians believe Jesus has.
- The Holy Spirit, active in the Old Testament, is now sent by Jesus to complete his work on earth.

An excellent site to explore ideas, facts and images of Jesus is
www.rejesus.co.uk

Symbols of the Holy Spirit in Christian art can be found at
www.st-andrews.ac.uk/institutes/itia/holy_spirit.html

WEBLINKS

3

KEY WORDS

Baptism – a ceremony of pouring water over a person, or being immersed in a pool of water. This symbolises an old life dying, a new one rising, and spiritual cleansing for the soul.

Confession – owning up to what we have done wrong.

Gehenna – the Hebrew word for hell in the gospels. A symbolic reference to a valley outside Jerusalem where rubbish was burnt. Jesus used this as an image for judgement.

Grace – undeserved favour from God.

Mortal sin – sin that is serious and deadly to the soul.

Original sin – a condition stemming from the disobedience of Adam and Eve, though there are different understandings of what has been passed down.

Purgatory – Roman Catholic belief in a place of preparation for heaven for those who are saved.

Reconciliation – making peace between two parties; also a sacrament where a person confesses before a priest.

Repentance – 'turning' from sin and wrong ways.

Salvation – mending a broken relationship, setting free, acceptance and healing.

Sin – 'missing the mark', falling short of what is right.

Structural sin – inherited wrong in systems and social structures that keep injustice going.

Venial sin – less serious sin that is not so hurtful.

SIN

KEY QUESTION

What is a sin and how can people be forgiven?

For Christians, **sin** means to turn from God and put yourself first, in the sense of being self-centred and therefore careless about the needs and feelings of others. The Greek word for sin in the New Testament is *hamartia*, which means 'to miss the mark'. This suggests that people are not fulfilling God's goals or their own.

A sin is not just an individual action, but the inner attitude of the person who does it, and the effect on other people. It means to go against what a person feels to be right, wilfully, and to hurt someone else in some way.

A parable

Many Christians see the story of Adam and Eve as symbolic of the meaning of sin. The couple are placed in the Garden of Eden, a paradise where they have all kinds of trees to eat from, including the Tree of Life. They are told that they must not eat from one tree – the Tree of Knowledge of Good and Evil. The serpent, representing evil, tempts them to eat from the forbidden tree, and they are changed inside. They are no longer conscious of God's care and love, and start to scheme to cover up their disobedience. God finds them out, and banishes them from Eden to the world outside, where life will be hard. This is known as 'the Fall' (i.e. the fall into sin).

The Tree of Life stands for the path of life and goodness. The Tree of Knowledge stands for the path of death and destruction. Adam and Eve

▲ A painting of Adam and Eve being expelled from Paradise, by Masaccio.

Original sin

KEY QUESTION

What is original sin?

Christians also talk about **original sin**. There are many different interpretations of this. Here are three:

- A common view is that 'original sin' was a moral stain passed down through the generations from Adam and Eve's first sin. Therefore, people were born with a wicked streak in their genes, somehow.
- Orthodox Christians believe Adam's fall led to mortality – death and suffering. There is no moral taint handed down, but our mortality makes us morally weak and it is a struggle to be good. We are not to blame for Adam's sin, but we suffer the consequences.
- Others do not believe that there ever was an Adam or Eve: they are just symbols of humans being confronted by the choice between good and evil. For them, original sin means the negative influence in the world that is built up over the ages from all the individual sins of people, which starts to work on people from birth, turning them away from good and dragging them down. It does not matter if this started with an original human couple or not, for it was started by someone, somewhere, and carries on. This is why it is often hard to do what you think is right, and, even worse, it might blind people to what is right. This is the state of things we are born into.

Literal readings of the Adam and Eve story suggest that we die because of that first sin. Others have a different view. Perhaps death is meant to be in God's plan, and is not a curse. We die to make room for others, and to move on, closer to God. Our sinfulness makes it something to fear, though, when it should be a letting go, a door opening to eternal life.

disobey God and become selfish, caring for their own desires only. Things start to go wrong; they feel guilty, and then life gets hard.

Venial and mortal sin

Roman Catholic Christians talk about two different types of sin, **venial** and **mortal**:

- *Venial sins* (e.g. telling a lie) are not as serious. A person can confess these privately to God, though they can also be confessed to a priest if this is more helpful.
- *Mortal sins* (e.g. murder) seriously affect a person's relationship with God, and the Roman Catholic Church teaches that these must be confessed to a priest. The priest, who speaks with the authority of Christ, will be able to help the person to receive God's forgiveness, despite his or her guilty feelings.

a What sense do many Christians make of the Adam and Eve story today? Say what the different details, such as the Tree of Knowledge, can stand for.

b Using a video camera, ask a selection of people around the school what they think sin is. Then ask what sins they think are really hard to forgive. Edit into this headlines from newspapers about crimes and atrocities. Then show a cross. Place around this the cuttings and add the words 'Forgive us our sins as we forgive those who sin against us.'

TEST YOURSELF

1 What does 'sin' mean?
2 What is the difference between mortal and venial sin?
3 Three definitions of original sin are provided here. What are they?

SALVATION

KEY QUESTION

What does it mean, 'to be saved'?

Sin is falling short of God's standards, and going against what a person feels to be right; a broken relationship results. There is a break in the relationship with God, with anyone the person has hurt and with the person's own self.

Salvation means turning to God and being open to God. This involves **repentance**, a word that means 'turning away' from wrong behaviour and ideas. Christians feel that a healing process begins as the relationship is restored. There is a feeling of being forgiven, of peace of mind and a resulting openness and friendliness to others – a person wants what is best for them, and is not just thinking of himself. Salvation is about being made a whole person, a complete human being, at peace with oneself, others, and with God. Christians believe that God comes to people's aid, as they are not strong-willed enough to save themselves. God moves towards us by **grace** (undeserved favour) when we have done nothing to earn it. We stand, in our moral failures, guilty before God and only his standard is good enough. Yet, Jesus brings forgiveness and makes us acceptable. God throws us a spiritual lifeline and our responsibility is to catch it. Salvation – being made whole – is a lifelong process, though, and not only a split second affair. It can begin in a blinding flash, a powerful moment of conversion, but it has to carry on growing.

Some Christians feel this process begins with **baptism** (see pp105–106).

Social liberation

Christians do not think that salvation only comes to people, but to society as well. Sin can exist in systems and structures of society. This is called **structural sin**. For example, the old political system of apartheid in South Africa encouraged racism against blacks. Or, think of the unfair trading system that makes developing countries poorer and leaves them with vast debts. Christians believe that salvation needs to affect structures such as these to help people to be free.

These structures were all started by individuals, but they have a life of their own, in a way, as the sin carries on from generation to generation in the systems people created. People are caught up in them and affected by them. Most Christians feel that these structures should be challenged by prayer and non-violent protest, but some are prepared to use violence in extreme situations if people are suffering greatly. People can co-operate with God in bringing salvation to the world – but their hearts must be changed first.

A Restored Relationship...

Selfishness and thoughtlessness can break relationships. 'Salvation' comes through a turning point, a sorrow for what has been wrong, and a working at a new relationship. There needs to be forgiveness to allow this to get started. Just as with everyday human life, so Christians believe that God works in our hearts to forgive, turn from sin and heal.

Write a story about a broken and restored relationship in everyday life – this can be based upon a true story or made up by you. Show how 'salvation' comes to someone.

What is being protested about here? Why would Christians say that this is a result of structural sin?

Reconciliation and forgiveness

John Bunyan imagined a scene in *The Pilgrim's Progress* that depicts what it is like to be forgiven. Pilgrim carries a heavy sack on his back. No one can tell him how to get rid of this until he climbs a hill and looks at the cross. The ties that bind the sack to him come loose and it rolls away down the hill. He is relieved and joyful, delighted to be free.

> He ran thus till he came at a place somewhat ascending; and upon that place stood a Cross, and a little below in the bottom, a sepulchre. So I saw in my dream, that just as Christian came up with the Cross, his burden loosed from off his shoulders, and fell from off his back; and began to tumble, and so continued to do till it came to the mouth of the sepulchre, where it fell in, and I saw it no more.
>
> Then was Christian glad and lightsome, and said with a merry heart, 'He hath given me rest, by his sorrow, and life, by his death.'
>
> *John Bunyan*, The Pilgrim's Progress

Forgiveness involves a letting go. It involves repentance, a turning away or around. If we forgive someone else, then we let go of our anger and desire to see that person punished. If we are forgiven, we let go of our guilty feelings.

It is not always easy and it can involve a struggle and some deep feelings. Christians believe that Jesus forgave people their sins and showed how much God loves humanity by dying on the cross.

Jesus taught about forgiveness in many different ways. In Luke 7:36–50, Jesus welcomes a woman who weeps at his feet. His dinner hosts are scandalised. The woman was a prostitute. He tells them off for being hard-hearted and slow to forgive.

> Therefore, I tell you, her many sins have been forgiven – for she loved much. But he who has been forgiven little loves little.
>
> *Luke 7:47*

▲ A woman who has lived a sinful life washes Jesus' feet with her tears and dries them with her hair. The great love that she shows proves that her sins are forgiven.

▲ Imagine the weight that is lifted from your shoulders after being forgiven.

A New Approach – Christianity

Jesus also taught that there was no limit to the number of times you should forgive someone. In Matthew 18:21–22 Peter asks if he should forgive someone as many as seven times. Jesus replies, 'I tell you, not seven times, but seventy-seven times.' In Jewish thought, this meant there was no limit. Seven as the perfect number, and seven times seven was infinite and endless.

Jesus lived out his teaching. On the cross, he prayed for his tormentors, 'Father, forgive them, for they do not know what they are doing' (Luke 23:34).

Forgiveness in Church

Reconciliation means when two people make peace with each other and restore their relationship. A person can offer forgiveness from his or her own heart, but this might not be received.

Some churches have the sacrament of reconciliation (also called 'Penance' or '**Confession**') to help people restore their relationship with God. People can say private prayers of confession to God, and there is often an opportunity to join in a form of general confession in a service (everyone says sorry together). Sometimes a more personal form of confession is needed to quieten the conscience. This is done to a priest or a minister in absolute secrecy or confidentiality. A declaration of forgiveness will be given to the penitent (the confessing person). This is also called the absolution, from the verb 'absolve', which means 'to set free from'.

A penance might be given – a prayer to say, an action, or a passage to read. This helps people to appreciate forgiveness. The penance might be to urge the penitent to go and make peace with someone he or she has hurt.

The Orthodox Churches teach that you should go to confession before receiving communion. The Roman Catholic Church teaches that it is only essential when you have committed a serious, mortal sin, though people are expected to go before Christmas and Easter. The Anglican Church teaches that it is freely available but there must be no compulsion – 'all may, none must, some should'.

Free Churches believe in the principle of sometimes confessing sins to trusted fellow believers, whether the minister or pastor or not. They follow the letter of James. They understand this to mean anyone, any believer, and not just a leader.

Therefore confess your sins to each other and pray for each other so that you may be healed.

James 5:16a

▲ A confession today can be made face to face with a priest.

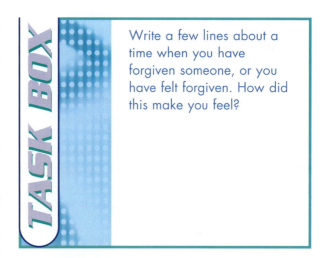

TASK BOX

Write a few lines about a time when you have forgiven someone, or you have felt forgiven. How did this make you feel?

THE LIFE EVERLASTING

> ### KEY QUESTION
>
> What do Christians believe about the afterlife?

The Bible presents a number of striking images of the life of the world to come, or the 'afterlife' as it is more commonly known. It is described as a state of bliss or glory. Some passages have ranks of singing angels, shining light, dazzling objects and magnificent colours:

> At once I was in the Spirit, and there before me was a throne in heaven with someone sitting on it. And the one who sat there had the appearance of jasper and carnelian. A rainbow, resembling an emerald, encircled the throne. ... From the throne came flashes of lightning, rumblings and peals of thunder. Before the throne, seven lamps were blazing. These are the seven spirits of God. Also before the throne there was what looked like a sea of glass, clear as crystal.
>
> *Revelation 4:2–3, 5–6*

This passage gives a disturbing feeling of the terrible and utter strangeness of the presence of God in heaven. It should not be taken literally for it is a piece of poetry. It is full of symbols:

- The lights (rainbow, the gleaming face, torches) suggest God's purity and goodness.
- The noises (thunder, rumblings, lightning) suggest tremendous power.
- The throne also suggests power and authority.
- The sea of glass suggests truth, beauty and purity.

The passage goes on to describe four living creatures that surround the throne – they suggest the terrifying otherness of God, a force beyond description.

All the descriptions of the afterlife in the Bible are poetic or symbolic because such a state of existence is beyond human knowledge and imagination. St Paul believed that the afterlife would come as a surprise and be beyond people's wildest dreams.

> No eye has seen,
>   no ear has heard,
> no mind has conceived
>   what God has prepared for those who love him.
>
> *1 Corinthians 2:9*

In the past, many people believed heaven was up above the sky somewhere, and that a person's spirit floated up to be with God. Some Jews believed that, instead of this, the dead were raised up in new bodies and lived on a renewed earth where there was no more death or suffering. Both of these ideas can be found in different parts of the Bible, although the writers are careful to stress that 'the life of the world to come' was really beyond description, and they were just using symbols to express it.

St Paul seemed to combine these two ideas into one idea of being raised up in a new body to a spiritual place. He talked about a 'spiritual body' (read 1 Corinthians 15:35–54).

Many Christians believe a person has an immortal soul, and that this lives on after the death of the body, as a mind, or in a new

TASK BOX

Read the passage written by St Paul below. What did he believe about resurrection? What do you think is meant by a 'spiritual body'?

So will it be with the resurrection of the dead. The body that is sown is perishable, it is raised imperishable; it is sown in dishonour, it is raised in glory; it is sown in weakness, it is raised in power; it is sown a natural body, it is raised a spiritual body.

1 Corinthians 15:42–4

spiritual body of some kind. Modern science cannot prove or disprove the idea of an immortal soul.

Some Christians think, however, that the immortal soul idea is wrong, and that our minds and feelings are a part of the working of the brain. Resurrection for them means that God creates a new life for people. God has had their individual personality stored in his memory, like a musical composer who remembers the notes of a piece and can get musicians to produce the sounds again. This way, there is nothing in people that automatically survives death: the afterlife is an act of God.

Modern Christians are influenced both by the biblical images and by modern scientific knowledge. They tend to believe a person lives on spiritually with God in another level or dimension of reality, beyond this physical universe. What shape or form this has, if any, is unknowable. This is the modern version of the 'floating up to the spirit-in-the-sky' idea. The soul, or personality, lives on in a new, spiritual body.

The modern Christian version of living on a renewed earth echoes what some scientists are suggesting: that the universe will stop expanding and may collapse in on itself, which will push matter out again in a new creation, with a new and possibly very different universe forming. This might be the new earth promised in poetic passages like Revelation 21:1; 'Then I saw a new heaven and a new earth, for the first heaven and the first earth had passed away ...'

TEST YOURSELF

1 What is meant by an 'immortal soul'?

2 Can there be an afterlife if we do not have an immortal soul?

PERSPECTIVES

Consciousness brings the mind alive; it is the ultimate puzzle to the neuroscientist. It is your most private place. This ultimate puzzle ... is perhaps a good place for any purely scientific survey, namely one of objective facts, to cease.

Susan Greenfield, The Human Brain: A Guided Tour

Dr Greenfield is an expert on the make-up of the brain but she admits that no one understands what makes us a conscious, thinking, feeling person. What is the real 'you' inside your head? Whether people call it soul, spirit or mind, it is a puzzle. It cannot be dissected under a microscope.

- Take a few moments and reflect upon your private feelings and beliefs. What is it that makes you 'you'?
- Play the 'Who are you?' game with a partner. Take it in turns to ask each other 'Who are you?' over and over again, volunteering any pieces of information you can think of. When do you run out of things to say? What is left unsaid?

KEY QUESTION

What do Christians believe about heaven, hell and purgatory?

▲ **A 15th century painting of the Last Judgement with Christ returning in glory. Who is seated around him and how are the people being raised reacting?**

Christians feel that God cannot let evil go unpunished, or suffering not atoned for. Otherwise, God would not be just and fair. This is the origin of ideas of hell and of punishment in the next life. In the book of Daniel in the Old Testament, some are raised to eternal life, but others are raised to eternal disgrace. In the Synoptic Gospels (Matthew, Mark and Luke), Jesus talked about the fire of hell (see Matthew 5:22, for example).

> If anyone's name was not found written in the book of life, he was thrown into the lake of fire.
>
> *Revelation 20:15*

This gave rise to the idea of hell as a terrible place of fire and eternal torture. Both Jesus and the early Church taught that Hell was a reality; that we did have to face judgement, and that some people would refuse God's love. We have the gift of free will; we are free to say 'Yes' or 'No' to God for all eternity.

Some modern Christians feel very uncomfortable with this idea of hell, though. If God is a God of love, how could he reject people in such a cruel and final way? God would then be responsible for running an eternal Chamber of Horrors. The Bible verses might not have meant such an idea, however. How literal or symbolic were they meant to be?

- They were symbolic. The fire suggests God's power and anger purifying sin, as rubbish burnt up by flames, or germs killed off by heat. The word for 'hell' in the gospels is **Gehenna** (in the Hebrew), a symbolic reference to the Valley of Hinnom outside Jerusalem where the city's rubbish was burned. Jesus used this as an image of God's coming judgement; he did not mean it to be taken literally. *Hell is therefore a state of being cut off from God, and not a place of physical flames.*

- The Bible language is open to interpretation – is the purpose of the 'fire' for punishment or for correction? If for correction, then it has the idea of God purifying the evil out of sinners to make them worthy of living in his Kingdom. Some wonder if hell is a temporary state, a place of purification to make people sorry for their sins and ready for heaven. When the Bible speaks of evil being destroyed forever, it need not mean the person, but their sin. Others reject this, pointing out that the fire of God in the Bible is usually an image of judgement, and not of purification, and people really can refuse God's offer of love forever.

- Many Christians believe that *it is people themselves who put themselves into hell*, and not God. At the Judgement, all they have done and all that they are is revealed to them, and some will not be able to stand it. The presence of God's holy light will be a burning fire to them and a joy to others.

The Roman Catholic Church developed a belief in **purgatory**. People in purgatory are saved, but have to be prepared for heaven. In medieval times, it was a place of less suffering than hell. Now, Catholics see this as being purified and healed by the love of God.

Modern Christians stress the love of God and the fact that he will not easily give up on anyone he has created. While there is anything in a person that can be redeemed they are redeemable and not lost for ever.

The parable of the Last Judgement in Matthew 25:31–46 draws together many of these themes. The righteous stand on the right-hand side of the Son of Man (Jesus) when he returns to judge the earth and are sent into the blessed Kingdom. The unrighteous are sent into the 'eternal fire which has been prepared for the Devil and his angels' (Matthew 25:41). This is after the inner motives and deeds of all concerned have been revealed: some visited Christ (in other humans) when he was sick, hungry or naked; others closed their hearts to their fellow humans.

It is possible to interpret this parable in the old way – God sending some into eternal damnation – or to see it in a more modern light – of people's own consciences casting them into the purifying fire, running away from the holy love of God.

The parable also points out that salvation was not only for those who called themselves Christians, but for those who 'did the will of God' by being open to their neighbour. Hence, many Christians believe that there is a place in the Kingdom for many members of other faiths, and for many who have not even believed in God on earth, but have unknowingly done his will in various ways.

TEST YOURSELF

1 What is meant by purgatory?
2 Which Christians believe in this?
3 What did Jesus say about *Gehenna*?
4 What hope does the parable of the sheep and the goats give to people who have not believed in this life?

A site dealing with near-death experiences and ideas of heaven is at
⚫ www.bbc.co.uk/schools/gcsebitesize/sosteacher/re/37370.shtml

WEBLINKS

REMEMBER

- Christians believe that everyone has sinned in some way.
- God is graceful and takes the initiative to restore the relationship with us.
- People can begin to turn towards God through baptism and in their hearts.
- The sacrament of reconciliation exists to help people find forgiveness when they cannot quieten their own conscience.

1 Describe what Christians believe about repentance. [8]
2 Explain the different beliefs Christians have about confession. [7]
3 'Not all sins can be forgiven.' Do you agree? Give reasons to support your answer showing that you have considered other points of view. [5]
4 What do Christians believe about heaven? [6]
5 What is purgatory, and which group of Christians believe in this? [4]
6 'Once you are dead, you are dead!'
   Do you agree with this? Give reasons to support your point of view and show that you have considered those of others. Make sure you refer to Christian beliefs. [5]

Assignment

KEY WORDS

Apostolic – based upon the teaching of the apostles.

Beatitudes – 'happy sayings'. A list of nine sayings of Jesus about lifestyles.

Canonisation – the process of making someone a saint in the Roman Catholic Church.

Liberation theology – a movement that seeks to apply Christian teaching to society and to champion the cause of the poor.

Saint – 'one set apart', the name for any believer in the New Testament but often used of a specially holy believer.

Torah – the Law of Moses found in the first five books of the Old Testament.

THE SERMON ON THE MOUNT

Two passages of teaching from Jesus are going to be studied.

▲ 1. Jesus taught that wrong actions are the result of wrong attitudes and feelings.

2. Murder starts with anger and rage when it all gets out of hand.

3. Adultery begins with a lustful glance, wanting to use someone for your pleasure.

4. Jesus taught that people should repay evil with good rather than trying to hurt them back.

5. Jesus said that our inner intentions matter more than actions, sometimes. If you give a charity a large amount of money but make a show of it, this is not as good as someone who gives a small amount in secret.

6. Money is OK if used wisely and not made into a god.

7. Jesus taught people not to judge others. If you point a finger at someone, always remember that you have three others pointing back at you!

The Sermon on the Mount (Matthew 5–7) is a collection of various sayings of Jesus that he probably spoke on separate occasions, but the Gospel writer has put them together to form a summary of Jesus' moral teaching. It is called the Sermon on the Mount because the writer introduces it with Jesus going up a hill to teach his disciples. This would have been very significant for a Jew at the time, for Moses received the Law (**Torah**) of God on Mount Sinai. Jesus was thus giving a new law.

The Sermon falls into two sections: the Beatitudes, and teaching about various topics.

The Beatitudes (Matthew 5:3–15)

These are short sayings, and there are nine of them. '**Beatitude**' means 'happy saying'. Jesus explains that for a truly happy lifestyle we must be honest and not give in when the going gets tough. Being happy, for Jesus, did not mean being lazy, well-off and selfish. It is virtuous, and of a clean conscience. God's blessing rests upon such people. The word 'blessing' and 'to be happy' are related; they both come from the Latin word *beatus*:

1 *Blessed are the poor in spirit …*
2 *Blessed are those who mourn …*
3 *Blessed are the meek …*
4 *Blessed are those who hunger and thirst for righteousness …*
5 *Blessed are the merciful …*
6 *Blessed are the pure in heart …*
7 *Blessed are the peacemakers …*
8 *Blessed are those who are persecuted because of righteousness …*
9 *Blessed are you when people insult you, persecute you and falsely say all kinds of evil against you because of me.*

The first three Beatitudes are reversals of traditional expectations. They sound strange at first. Jesus means that people who know their needs, who are not locked up in themselves and cold to others, will be truer human beings. They can feel, hope and love. They will be more open to God, too, than someone who feels self-sufficient, or who manipulates others.

Beatitudes 5 and 6 are about a true search for God and its rewards, and 4 and 7 are about a true search for justice. 'Pure in heart' means to have singleness of vision, not being distracted by selfish concerns.

Beatitudes 8 and 9 are about suffering at the hands of others for doing what you believe to be right. If people suffer in this way, they are counted 'happy' because they are keeping their integrity and God will reward them. The only difference between 8 and 9 is that 9 speaks specifically about being persecuted for being a follower of Jesus.

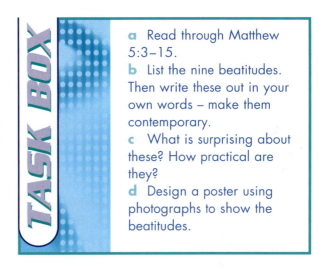

TASK BOX

a Read through Matthew 5:3–15.
b List the nine beatitudes. Then write these out in your own words – make them contemporary.
c What is surprising about these? How practical are they?
d Design a poster using photographs to show the beatitudes.

The rest of the Sermon concerns teaching on the Jewish Law, anger, adultery, divorce, vows, revenge and love of enemies, charity, prayer and fasting, riches and possessions, and judging others.

The Law (Matthew 5:17–20)

Jesus said he had come to make the teachings of the Law come true. He seems to be saying that all its commandments are to be kept, but he ignored the food laws (like not eating pork) when he taught, for example, that it did not matter what food you ate. It is the state of a person's heart that makes them 'clean' or 'unclean' (see Mark 7:14).

It is difficult to know what he meant by the Law not being done away with, but perhaps he meant that all its commandments of love were eternal and could not be cancelled. On another occasion he summed up the Old Testament Law as being love of God and love of neighbour. That was what really mattered.

Anger (Matthew 5:21–6)

Jesus teaches that what is in a person's mind and feelings is the real issue. He points out that anger in itself can be dangerous, as it can lead to murder. The Old Testament Law dealt only with the act of murder, not the inward feeling of hating someone. Other people should not be treated as 'good-for-nothings' because all are the children of God. On another occasion, though, Jesus himself showed anger, when he cleared the traders out of the Temple (see Mark 11:15–19); perhaps righteous anger, speaking out against injustices, is all right, but not anger that hates someone else and might secretly want to see them dead.

Adultery (Matthew 5:27–30)

Again, Jesus goes behind the outward action and points to what a person is thinking or feeling inside. Adultery, strictly speaking, means married people having sex with someone other than their spouse. But adultery starts with a lustful look. Jesus did not just understand sin as wrong actions, but also as the wrong thoughts that start these off. He might have been speaking tongue in cheek, here, for many married people have cast a lustful look at someone in their life! He was telling people to keep their thoughts in check, but, perhaps, also, he was warning people not to be too judgemental of those who committed adultery. It is a weakness many people can fall into if they are not careful, and people should not pretend to be righteous and condemn others when they often feel the same way inside. The story in John 8:1–11 shows Jesus being very understanding and forgiving to a woman caught in the act of adultery. In no way was he condoning it, though. There is nothing wrong with sexual desire; it is natural, but lust means wanting to use someone rather than wanting to love them. It means caring more about selfish pleasure than the whole quality of a relationship. Adultery breaks the trust in a marriage, after all.

Divorce (Matthew 5:31–2)

The Law of Moses allowed divorce if a man found something shameful in his wife. There were two schools of thought about the meaning of this. One school claimed it meant anything that displeased the husband, such as the wife being a bad cook, or always nagging; the other said it referred to adultery.

Jesus sided with this second school and allowed divorce only if adultery was involved. Some Christians today feel that if Jesus said that one thing could break a marriage, then there might be other serious things that could, like cruel treatment or desertion. They follow Jesus' teaching that divorce should not be a cheap and easy option, however. There are different views about this between Churches. The Roman Catholic Church, for example, interprets this passage to mean that even adultery cannot justify divorce.

Vows (Matthew 5:33–7)

Jewish people at the time made many promises by swearing oaths. People were more superstitious about such things then, and it was a way of trying to persuade someone you were telling the truth, or even a way of trying to cover up a lie. The name of God was often used in these oaths, which Jesus found to be offensive. He taught that God's name should not be dragged into petty disputes; people should speak the truth plainly and say what they mean.

Revenge and love of enemies (Matthew 5:38–48)

Jesus went beyond the strict letter of an Old Testament law. Many Rabbis felt uneasy about applying 'an eye for an eye' literally, preferring a payment of compensation. Jesus based the command to love one another on Leviticus 19:18 ('love your neighbour as yourself'). Hating the enemy was not necessarily a part of Jewish tradition, but was a common human failing. There was a debate among some people, though, about just who their neighbour was. Did this include foreigners or just the Jews? Hence the question put to Jesus that inspired the

A New Approach – Christianity

parable of the Good Samaritan ('Who is my neighbour?' Luke 10:30-37). Jesus wants love to be shown to offenders, whatever their creed or ethnic origin. This should have more power to change them.

Many Christians argue that the purpose of prison sentences should be to try to reform the criminal, and not to hurt him or her. But they also feel that letting an enemy insult you personally is one thing (you can take it), but if other people are threatened it is a different matter. Hence, if a criminal will not respond to reform, he or she must be locked away for the protection of society.

Charity, prayer and fasting (Matthew 6:1–18)

Jesus criticises people who make a show of religion, telling people how good they are: some giving to the poor only in public, so all can see; some praying on street corners, so all can hear; some going around in sackcloth when they fast, so everyone will know. Jesus advises people to give money in secret, to pray in secret and to dress normally and be cheerful when fasting, so no one else knows. He teaches that it is sincerity that matters, not the actions of giving to charity, praying or fasting in themselves.

Jesus also teaches that prayer should be to the point, and not be said like a form of magic that uses a great number of phrases, thinking you are more likely to be heard that way. It is here that Matthew inserts the Lord's Prayer, with its themes of God as a loving Father, of hope for the Kingdom and forgiveness of one's enemies.

Riches and possessions (Matthew 6:19–24)

Jesus teaches that true riches are spiritual realities because these last for ever. Values such as love and freedom are more important than having plenty of money. People are easily tempted to give up their values if they will benefit financially, such as walking over others to get to the top, taking bribes, or fighting to keep their possessions. Jesus sees a life spent on earning wealth as a waste of time if spiritual values are ignored. He points out that money can easily become an idol, to be worshipped rather than God. If money becomes a person's

TASK BOX

What insights would the Sermon on the Mount (described on the following page) give us about these scenes?

Christian beliefs about how Christians should live

master, then it will make the person selfish. It is all right to have money, however, so long as it is used wisely: money should be a servant, not a master.

Judging others (Matthew 7:1–6)

Jesus warns that if people are quick to accuse someone else of a failing, then they are forgetting that they are only human, too. When they point a finger at someone, three are pointing back at them! No one is perfect. This should make people more sensitive to each other, and more ready to forgive. This is not to say that you should never speak out, but it is a general principle for Christians to remember, because it keeps things in perspective: 'There but for the grace of God go I.'

The teaching in the Sermon on the Mount is a summary of a Christian lifestyle. Some of the details and circumstances in the teaching of Jesus here are perhaps irrelevant and out of date because he was dealing with certain situations in first-century Galilee and Judea – like people standing on street corners to say their prayers, or the teaching about oaths. But there are eternal principles contained within these teachings that Christians believe still apply today:

- Sin is not just a wrong action, but the inner feelings and thoughts of the person are involved, too. That's where people have to change. This teaching may also make it hard to say what is sinful in every situation. For example, supposing a woman, trying to bring up a baby on her own and suffering from lack of money, stress and isolation on a large housing estate, batters her baby – is she really to blame when she is so affected by her circumstances?
- Sincerity is what matters in religion, not how well prayers are said, nor how often people fast, nor how much they give to charity. A person who hardly knows any prayers but who says them with meaning is worth more to God than experts who can recite long prayers full of long words, but do not say them from the heart.
- People should strive for peace, and develop a forgiving attitude, remembering that they often do wrong, too.
- People should not be self-centred but be open to others and to God. That way they will find true happiness.

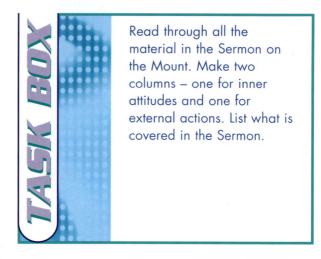

TASK BOX

Read through all the material in the Sermon on the Mount. Make two columns – one for inner attitudes and one for external actions. List what is covered in the Sermon.

THE GREAT COMMANDMENT

One of the teachers of the law came and heard [Jesus and the Sadducees] debating. Noticing that Jesus had given them a good answer, he asked him, 'Of all the commandments, which is the most important?'

'The most important one,' answered Jesus, 'is this: "Hear, O Israel, the Lord our God, the Lord is one. Love the Lord your God with all your heart and with all your soul and with all your mind and with all your strength." The second is this: "Love your neighbour as yourself." There is no commandment greater than these.'

'Well said, teacher,' the man replied. 'You are right in saying that God is one and there is no other but him. To love him with all your heart, with all your understanding and with all your strength, and to love your neighbour as yourself is more important than all burnt offerings and sacrifices.'

When Jesus saw that he had answered wisely, he said to him, 'You are not far from the kingdom of God.' And from then on no one dared ask him any more questions.

Mark 12:28–34

A teacher of the Law of Moses asked Jesus which commandment was the most important of all. There were 613 laws in the Law of Moses. (The Law ordered a number of rituals to be followed and also commanded spiritual things, such as worshipping only one God.) Jesus replied that the greatest commandment was to love God with all one's heart, soul, mind and strength, and that the second most important commandment was to love one's neighbour as oneself. The first is from Deuteronomy 6:4–5, and the second is from Leviticus 19:18 (both are books of the Torah, or Law).

Here, Jesus showed his skill in dealing with the Old Testament scripture, drawing out what he saw as its central teaching – love. Love of God and love of humanity cannot be separated. They are two sides of the same coin.

The teacher was pleased with this answer, and agreed that love was more important than the other commandments that ordered various types of sacrifices. Jesus told him he was not far from the Kingdom of God.

Jesus set aside many of the commandments in the Law, such as the food laws, but he regarded himself as a faithful Jew. It is likely that there were a number of Jews who thought that the spiritual commandments of the Law were more important than the ritualistic laws about sacrifice and diet, and that Jesus sided with them. He might have been more radical in his dismissal of some aspects of the Law, though, and probably believed he had the authority to do this as the Messiah.

SAINTS

KEY QUESTION
Who is a saint?

▲ Christian icon paintings represent saints with light around them and shining from their bodies to symbolise the presence of God in their lives. Orthodox Christians have a saying, 'The Lord is wonderful in his saints'. This is St Nicholas.

The word **saint** means someone who is holy, or set apart for God. In this sense, all Christians who believe that God's Spirit is at work within them are saints, even though they are far from perfect. The New Testament uses the word saint for any believer.

a Write out the Great Commandment.
b Look up Deuteronomy 6:4–5 and Leviticus 19:18 in the Hebrew Bible.
c Why are the two sections of the Great Commandment like two different sides of the same coin?

'Communion of saints' means the fellowship of all Christians, alive and dead. Christians are part of a family, or a community, of believers. They are not meant to be loners. They believe they share the life of Christ through the Spirit. Christians do not think that death stops their sharing in Christ's life, or with one another. It all carries on, for eternity.

When Christians usually talk about saints, however, they mean especially holy people who lived lives very close to God and who set examples for others to follow.

Roman Catholic, Orthodox and some Anglican Christians believe that they can ask the saints in heaven to pray for them, just as a Christian might ask someone on earth to pray for them if they are going through a difficult time. The saints are thought to be closer to God, and therefore their prayers are stronger. Mary, the mother of Jesus, is honoured above all the other saints because she gave birth to the Redeemer, and is thought to be especially close to him.

In the Orthodox Church there is a saying, 'The Lord is wonderful in his saints!' This means that the saints present God to people by setting an example and letting God shine through their lives. The Eastern churches have paintings, holy icons or images. These are special, painted images on wood of the saints that not only have a halo of light around their heads, but also have light shining out from their faces in order to put the idea across of their being witnesses to the reality of God.

There is a touching but amusing story of a young child who was asked what a saint was. Thinking of the figures on the stained glass windows in the church, she replied, 'A saint is someone whom the light shines through!' In a spiritual sense, that is exactly what Christians believe a saint is.

A recent case of the canonisation of a saint by the Roman Church was that of Maximilian Kolbe, a Polish priest and member of the Franciscan order. He was in a concentration camp in 1941 when he volunteered to die in a punishment squad to let a married man with a family go free.

Some Christians started to be honoured as saints when they were martyred in the Roman Empire. A local cult of a martyr grew up around his or her homeland or place of death. The same honours were then extended to all outstanding Christians. The people mentioned by name in the New Testament were automatic candidates as they were close to Jesus.

The Roman Catholic Church has a complicated procedure for pronouncing people saints. It is called **canonisation** (which means formal admission to the list of saints). A case is heard for and against a person in a council held in the Vatican, and the Pope has the final word.

In the Orthodox Church, saints are pronounced by local councils of bishops. The Anglican Church honours the saints that were established before its split with Rome. It does not proclaim any new saints, though many people are honoured as saints unofficially, and special days to remember them are added to the Church's calendar.

Protestant Christians are wary of the cult of the saints. They feel that a person should pray to God through Jesus alone. Otherwise it might cause confusion and people might start to treat the saints as 'gods' themselves.

▲ Maximilian Kolbe

Other Churches would argue, however, that although it is true that some more superstitious believers might be afraid of approaching Jesus directly and prefer to go through a saint, this is certainly not the official doctrine of the cult of the saints. People can ask for their help, but they are not a substitute for Jesus. Jesus can still be approached directly, and should be.

Whatever beliefs people have about the saints, there are outstanding Christian men and women that all believers can admire.

TEST YOURSELF

1 Who are called saints in the New Testament?
2 What is canonisation?
3 How do eastern icons portray the saints?

Mother Teresa

Mother Teresa was born Agnes Gonxha Bojaxhiu in Yugoslavia in 1910 of Albanian parents. She was a Roman Catholic. She felt from the age of 12 that she wanted to give her life to God's service. When she was 17, she went to join the Loreto Nuns at their headquarters in Dublin, Ireland. She had heard about this group at school, and the work they did in India. After initial training in Ireland, she was sent to Darjeeling in India where she became a novice (a person training to be a nun). When she took her final vows to be a nun she took the name Teresa, after a favourite saint of hers.

She was then sent to Calcutta to teach geography in a school. The pupils were from rich families, and the work was easy. However, the school and the convent were in a poor part of the city. Many people lived out on the streets, in shelters made out of old boxes, or in rows of simple huts. These people had travelled into the city after famine had struck their village and were desperate for food and work. They begged what they could, and a few were lucky to earn a little money now and then. There were sick and elderly people just dying in the streets, with dogs and rats amongst them looking for food scraps.

Gradually, Teresa felt that she should leave the convent to work amongst the poor. It was two years before she was allowed to go. She had to train as a nurse with a different order of nuns, and then she returned to the city. A family gave her a room, and she started to tend sick people there. She taught the local slum children how to read, write and how to keep themselves clean. She held her classes in the street, drawing in the dust because there was no blackboard. Gradually, others joined her, and she called them her Sisters.

After five years of begging for medicines, and having no room to treat patients properly, she went to the Calcutta Council. They offered her an old rest room next to a Hindu temple where pilgrims used to rest. She moved in and began to take very sick people off the streets. She called the place *Nirmal Hriday*, 'Place of the Pure Heart'.

In 1950, she and her Sisters were allowed to form a new order, the Missionaries of Charity. More money was donated and more helpers came. Her work spread over India and the world with the creation of Homes for the Dying and Children's Homes, as well as Leprosy Homes. Mother Teresa's example seems to have sparked off compassion in many other people. She was awarded the Nobel Prize for Peace in 1979 and died in August 1997.

The Sisters do not try to convert people to

Christianity. There are daily services for the Sisters, and they will instruct people in the Christian faith if they desire it, but their job is to be helpers to anyone, no matter what their race or creed. The aim in the Homes for the Dying is to let people die in a loving environment, even if they have not known love at any other time in their lives. The motive for all their work can best be summed up in Mother Teresa's own words:

> Let no one ever come to you without going away better and happier. Let there be kindness in your face, kindness in your eyes. . . . In each suffering person you can see Jesus.
>
> *Mother Teresa*

Mother Teresa's story highlights the compassion Jesus showed for the poor and the social outcasts of his day. This love for other human beings is a central part of the Gospel message.

Mother Teresa's story highlights the issue of innocent suffering. The people she helped did nothing to deserve the troubles they faced. They were just unlucky being born where and when they were. Christianity teaches about a God of love, so why does this suffering go on in the world?

Christians have been trying to answer this question for ages. The usual answer is that human beings are a 'fallen' species. Basically, this means that they are out of tune with God because they often go their own selfish way. They are not functioning as they should be, and many things go wrong with the world. Wars and famines can be caused by humanity's own greed; they are not God's doing. God does not step in to force people to change, because he gives people free will, freedom to choose good or evil. God has sent teachers, and has come specially in Jesus, to teach people the way to live, but he will not force anyone to listen.

This means that we live in a world where things can and often do go wrong, where tragedies happen that are not part of God's plan for people. That is how the world is, but Christians like Mother Teresa feel it is their job to help people to feel the love of God in the midst of the problems of life, and to take courage and to work to make the world a better place.

Some are critical of charitable workers such as Mother Teresa, arguing that the structures of an unjust society need to be changed rather than constantly giving handouts to people. Others point out that structural sin does need to be addressed if there is to be any abiding change for the better, but in the meantime many people are suffering, and need immediate acts of compassion.

PERSPECTIVES

Mother Teresa's work can best be understood as an imitation of that of Jesus:

Christ's life was not written during his lifetime, yet he did the greatest work on earth. He redeemed the world and taught mankind to love his Father. The work is his work and to remain so, all of us are but his instruments who do our own little bit and pass by.
Mother Teresa

A New Approach – Christianity

TASK BOX

a Write a series of bullet points that summarise Mother Teresa's life and work.

b What strikes you most about her?

c How do some Christians respond to the question, 'Why does God allow suffering in the world?' How did Mother Teresa respond to this?

Hélder Câmara

Hélder Câmara was born in 1909 in Brazil. He was brought up as a Roman Catholic Christian and was ordained as a priest in 1931. He became a bishop in 1952 and was based in Rio de Janeiro. He was involved in setting up the National Conference of Brazilian Bishops and co-ordinated various other conferences. He became a well-known Church leader with weekly radio broadcasts and occasional television sermons.

Câmara spoke about the condition of the poor in a society that had a great divide between rich and poor, particularly in Rio. Playboy beaches were close to shanty towns and slum dwellers. In 1964 a military coup overthrew the government of President Joao Goulart. Just before this, Câmara was made Archbishop of Olinda and Recife, a poverty-stricken area of Brazil. The new Pope, Paul VI, was an old friend of Câmara and he supported him.

The new archbishop threw himself into social programmes and relief work for the poor. These were difficult times when the military government suspected such talk of social action and justice as Marxism. They harassed him, insulted him and probably set up machine-gun attacks on his residence to scare him into silence. He angered the government and local landlords in 1967 by arguing that unless the Church championed the poor, there would be a violent revolution by the disposed. He was not advocating this, just warning that it would happen. He survived these criticisms and retired as Archbishop in 1984. He died in 1999.

 When I give food to the poor they call me a saint. When I ask why the poor have no food, they call me a communist.

Hélder Câmara

Câmara attended the second Vatican Council in Rome during the 1960s, urging the bishops to champion the cause of the poor and to redistribute the wealth of the Church. He was part of a movement that became known as **liberation theology**. This sought to apply theological beliefs about God to everyday life, and to bother as much about the body as the soul.

Jesus of Nazareth was a humble preacher of love – of God and of humanity. He told his followers that they were not to lord it over people and boss them around:

> You know that those who are regarded as rulers of the Gentiles lord it over them, and their high officials exercise authority over them. Not so with you. Instead, whoever wants to become great among you must be your servant, and whoever wants to be first must be slave of all. For even the Son of Man

did not come to be served, but to serve, and to give his life as a ransom for many.
Mark 10:42–5

Jesus stood up and proclaimed this passage from the Old Testament in the synagogue in Nazareth:

The Spirit of the Lord is on me,
   because he has anointed me
   to preach good news to the poor.
He has sent me to proclaim freedom for the prisoners
   and recovery of sight for the blind,
to release the oppressed,
   to proclaim the year of the Lord's favour.
Luke 4:18–19

All of this seems a far cry from the Church of Christendom with its powerful, rich prince-bishops, and its attempts to force people into believing. It seems a far cry from a Church that sides with the government of the day and does not think anything should be done to change the conditions of the poor except for giving them handouts.

Liberation theology seeks to apply the gospel message to the society that people live in, and liberationists believe not only in the power of Christ to change people within, but also in his power to challenge unjust structures and systems in society.

The movement began in developing countries because of the poverty of many of their people. This poverty is not a result of their idleness, but of government and international corruption. Loans are made to the poor countries so long as they will produce certain crops for export, and that often means there is not enough farmland left to produce sufficient food for the people. Many of the rich landowners pay very low wages to their workers, too.

Many Christians in these countries are campaigning for social change, and they do not think that the gospel is just about personal salvation (where you go when you die). Jesus is seen as their brother, as a man sharing their oppression and struggling with them for change.

The most active political groups, however, are in the Roman Catholic Church. The Church has thousands of base communities all over South America. A base community (also known as a 'grass-roots community') means a friendly gathering of Christians, with or without a priest, in someone's home, or in a local hall. They pray, worship, study the Bible together, and work out how to help each other practically. They also organise protests against their local councils and the government. Some liberation theologians might mix the gospels with Marxism, but by no means all. Hélder Câmara certainly did not. In fact, he criticised both the USA and the USSR for being too 'enclosed and imprisoned in their egoism', meaning that they put themselves first.

Liberation theologians want to see a Church that is:

■ A more loving community, with no differences between rich and poor members.

TASK BOX

a Summarise Hélder Câmara's life and work in a series of bullet points.
b What did he refuse to ignore and what got him into trouble with the government and the local landlords?
c Write a fictional account of a meeting of a base community. What might they discuss and try to do as well as worshipping?
d Play a game with four groups. Each group is given three cards. The cards have different resources, such as crops or oil. Some of the cards are different for each group. They do not all have the same cards. Each group represents a nation. Work out different ways of getting the resources your group needs. If one group has more than enough crops, for example, then they can barter for a share of oil. What ways are there besides using force?

A New Approach – Christianity

▲ A base community (or 'grass-roots community') in South America.

- Less authoritarian, with the people helping to make decisions along with the priests and bishops, and taking part in services.
- Committed to social action as well as preaching about personal conversion.

TEST YOURSELF

1 What is liberation theology?
2 What is a base community?
3 Why are some nations much poorer than others?

Martin Luther King

Martin Luther King was born into a respectable family in Atlanta, Georgia, USA, in 1929. His father was a Baptist minister, and King was ordained a Baptist minister himself in 1947. He went on to study at Boston and Harvard universities and became a Doctor of Philosophy at the age of 26.

In his youth, he had been made aware of the racism in the USA when he was not allowed to

play with some white children along his street, and he remembered seeing the secret all-white organisation, the Ku Klux Klan, beating up blacks on the streets. When he became pastor of a church in Montgomery, Alabama, he became active in the National Association of Coloured People. In 1955, King became the president of another organisation, the Montgomery Improvement Association. This group led a boycott of the buses by all blacks for 382 days. This was over the arrest of an old black woman. She had refused to give up her seat on the bus to a white person because she was tired.

The civil rights movement was made up of people who wanted change in American society and equal rights for blacks. They pressed King to preach the use of violence, if necessary, to help change things more quickly. He refused, and followed a policy of non-violent protest. He would organise petitions, demonstrations and sit-ins, but there must be no violence. He took this both from the teachings of Jesus and from the Indian leader Gandhi, who had used non-violence to try to end the British occupation of India some years earlier.

King often suffered unfairly. Once, he was arrested for driving at 30mph in a 25mph area, his house was bombed, he was stabbed by an unstable black woman and he received many offensive phone calls or letters each day. Some white people felt angered and threatened by him; this was because he was making them face up to their prejudices and trying to get them to change their way of life.

In 1962, he met President Kennedy, and a year later, in August, he led a march on Washington of 250,000 people (60,000 of whom were whites). This was a demonstration in favour of the Civil Rights Bill being debated by Congress (the American Parliament). It was passed in 1964, but King did not think it went far enough. He carried on negotiations with the new President, Lyndon Johnson.

King was awarded the Nobel Peace Prize in 1964, and he donated the $54,000 to the civil rights movement. His life ended suddenly on 4 April 1968: he was shot in the head while standing on the balcony of his hotel in Memphis, Tennessee, by a sniper in the crowd.

He had succeeded in winning better conditions for the country's blacks, such as desegregated buses in areas of the South (blacks and whites used to have to sit separately). He summed up his work in a speech he made when he received the Nobel Prize for Peace:

> I have the audacity to believe that peoples everywhere can have three meals a day for their bodies, education and culture for their minds, and dignity, equality and freedom for their spirits. I believe that what self-centred men have torn down, other-centred men can build up. I still believe that one day mankind will bow before the altars of God and be crowned triumphant over war and bloodshed. ... I still believe that we shall overcome.
>
> *Martin Luther King*

King's story highlights the need some Christians feel to be involved in politics. They do not see Christianity as just being about saving people's souls to get them to heaven. An important part of the gospel message is love and justice for human beings. If things in society rob some people of love and justice, then these things are to be challenged. Politics is then brought in, because politicians have the power to change things.

Some Christians are wary of this; they think priests and pastors should stick to their prayers and leave social change to politicians and social workers. Other Christians feel they cannot help but be involved in politics if they really love their neighbours.

Some Christians feel it is sometimes right to use violence to stop a corrupt government, but King disagreed. He preferred non-violent action. The benefit of this is that you do not repay evil for evil, hurt for hurt, and that gains public support because it shows the authorities up for what they are. However, many people may suffer in the process and it may take a long time to win.

King's story also highlights that racism is anti-Christian because all races of people have been created by the same God and are equal in his sight.

A New Approach – Christianity

a Summarise Martin Luther King's life and work in a series of bullet points.

b 'You have heard that it was said, "Love your neighbour and hate your enemy." But I tell you: Love your enemies and pray for those who persecute you' (Matthew 5:43–4). How did Martin Luther King live out these words of Jesus?

c 'We shall overcome ...' Write a report about present-day struggles and human rights issues that need to be championed.

WEBLINKS

Sites for Maximilian Kolbe, Mother Teresa, Martin Luther King and Hélder Câmara can be found at:

🕷 www.catholic-forum.com/saints/saintm01.htm

🕷 www.tsas-re.freeserve.co.uk/teresa.html

🕷 www.spartacus.schoolnet.co.uk/usakingML.htm

🕷 www.saidwhat.co.uk/quotes/h/helder_camara_708.php

REMEMBER

▸ A saint is a believer, but outstanding believers are honoured and remembered.

▸ Love for God and for neighbour are what the commandments are all about.

▸ Following Jesus demands risk, challenge and examination of inner motives.

---

1 Describe what is taught about forgiveness in the Sermon on the Mount. [4]

2 Explain why Christians might want to help people who are convicted criminals. [6]

3 Explain what Christianity teaches about showing compassion for others. [6]

4 'Christians should avoid conflict at all cost.'
Do you agree? Give reasons for your opinion and show that you have considered other points of view. [4]

5 What is the Great Commandment? [8]

6 What did Jesus teach about hypocrisy and making a display of religion in the Sermon on the Mount? [7]

7 'Christians should not get involved in conflict or politics.'
Do you agree with this? Give reasons for your own point of view and show consideration for those of others. Mention ideas from the teaching of Jesus and from the life of one of the Christian leaders studied in this chapter. [5]

Assignment

KEY WORDS

Advent – from the Latin 'arrival'. The four Sundays before Christmas.

Christmas – 'the mass of Christ', celebrating the birth of Jesus.

Easter – the celebration of the resurrection of Jesus.

Epiphany – 'the appearance' of Jesus to the magi or wise men.

Good Friday – the day recalls Jesus' dying on the cross.

Holy Week – remembering the last week of Jesus' life.

Lent – the five weeks before Easter. A period of fasting and preparation.

Magi – the wise men, from 'magus', meaning wise person, usually a magician or stargazer.

Maundy Thursday – the day on which Jesus' washing of his disciples' feet and sharing of the Last Supper is commemorated.

Palm Sunday – the day that Jesus' entry into Jerusalem on a donkey is remembered.

Passion – the story of Jesus' journey to the cross.

Pentecost – the time when the gift of the Holy Spirit was given to the disciples.

Saturnalia – the pagan Roman New Year festival on 25 December.

Vigil – a late-night service of preparation.

Virgin Birth – the belief that Jesus was conceived in the womb of a virgin, Mary.

KEY QUESTION

What is the value of special festivals?

Events like birthdays and anniversaries are special occasions when something can be celebrated. When we celebrate birthdays we are giving thanks for the life of a friend or relative. A few people decide not to keep birthdays and similar times because they say that you should be thankful for a person's life all the year round. There is a point to this, but human nature being what it is, we do tend to take things and people for granted and get caught up in the ordinary events of everyday life.

Having special days on which to remember and celebrate things makes sure that we do take time to value people or memories. It also gives a pattern to the year, so that time does not just seem to flow by, and it gives people something to look forward to and to plan for. Celebrating a birthday or an anniversary or the New Year makes us take time to think about things and take stock of where we are and what we are doing. As these are specially set dates, the celebrations usually follow a ritual, such as giving cards and eating special food associated with the time, such as turkey at Christmas or cake on a birthday. These things are familiar and focus our mind on what is going on.

Christianity has specially set days and times to celebrate various events in its faith. There are three main times of celebration: **Christmas**, **Easter** and **Pentecost**. These are the festivals of the Church, and festivities suggest joy and a party spirit. Each of these has moments like a thanksgiving party, but there are serious moments and times of reflection, too. The three great festivals celebrate events in the life of Jesus and in the life of the Church:

- *Christmas* celebrates the birth of Christ.
- *Easter* celebrates the death and resurrection of Christ.
- *Pentecost* celebrates the gift of the Holy Spirit to the Church.

There are other joyful festivals, such as the **Epiphany**. This is when the star led the wise men to the baby Jesus.

There are also special times of preparation such as **Advent** and **Lent**. These are the seasons before Christmas and Easter.

KEY QUESTION

What does Christmas remember and how is this celebrated by Christians?

The story

The Christmas story is told in two of the Gospels: Matthew and Luke. The other two Gospels start their stories when Jesus is an adult. In both Matthew and Luke the story is that Jesus was born of a virgin mother as a result of a miracle. In Matthew's account (Matthew 1:20–1) an angel appeared to Joseph in a dream: 'Do not be afraid to take Mary home as your wife, because what is conceived in her is from the Holy Spirit. She will give birth to a son, and you are to give him the name Jesus, because he will save his people from their sins' (Matthew 1:20–1).

Luke tells the story from Mary's point of view. This is part of his description of Mary's encounter with an angel, an event known as the Annunciation: 'But the angel said to her, "Do not be afraid, Mary, you have found favour with God. You will be with child and give birth to a son, and you are to give him the name Jesus. He will be great and will be called the Son of the Most High" ' (Luke 1:30–2).

Matthew saw the miraculous birth as a fulfilment of an Old Testament prophecy in Isaiah 7:14. Matthew's version of the prophecy (1:23) is usually translated into English as, 'A virgin will become pregnant and have a son, and he will be called Immanuel (which means, "God is with us").'

Luke has the story of the angels appearing to the shepherds in the fields and telling them the good news that Christ had been born (2:8–20). Note that each Gospel tells only one of these stories, and they were combined by people in artwork later on.

Mary would have been a young girl when she gave birth, some think possibly between 14 and 16 years of age. According to Luke, she and Joseph had to travel to Bethlehem because of a census (a register of names) that was being taken by the Romans. There was no room to stay in any of the inns and so she had to give birth in a stable. Many Eastern stables are in caves, and are not too clean!

Whatever truth there is behind all these stories, it is a fact that Jesus was born. No one knows exactly when, though. It was in or before 4 BCE, because Matthew says that King Herod the Great was still alive at the time, and he died in 4 BCE. (If the story of the shepherds is anything to go by, he must have been born in spring, because they would have been out only at that time watching their flocks, because of the lambing season.)

December 25 was the date of a Roman festival called **Saturnalia**, which celebrated the sun god's victory over winter. When the Roman Empire accepted Christianity as its official religion in the fourth century CE, they stopped worshipping the sun god and made 25 December Jesus' official birthday. It seems that Christmas was not celebrated before this time, though.

TEST YOURSELF

1 Which Gospels tell the Christmas story?
2 When was Jesus born?
3 What was Saturnalia?

The celebrations

Christians celebrate Christmas in a number of ways. Roman Catholics and Anglicans keep the season of Advent. This is a time of preparation for four weeks before Christmas. Some churches light Advent wreaths that have four candles, one for each Sunday. Advent calendars will be kept in homes, each having 24 small card windows to be opened, day by day, through December until the 24th – Christmas Eve.

TASK BOX

a Which part of the Christmas story is being represented in this scene from Peru?
b Which parts of the story are told by Luke?
c Which parts are told by Matthew?
d Why were Christmas cribs first made?
e Are Christmas trees anything to do with the story of Jesus?

Christmas carols, special hymns about the birth of Jesus, will be sung, and some church groups will go singing around the streets. Children act out the story of the birth of Jesus in church or school. Crib scenes will be set up in homes and churches. At midnight on Christmas Eve many Christians will gather for a special service, or they may go to a family service on Christmas Day itself. The giving of presents remembers the visit of the wise men, and the great gift given to humanity in Jesus himself. Many homes and churches will have a Christmas crib showing the stable and the main characters in the Christmas story. Cribs were first introduced in the thirteenth century by St Francis of Asissi in Italy. He made these to teach the illiterate peasants all about the story.

Many of the other traditions surrounding the celebration of Christmas have got nothing to do with Christianity. Holly and mistletoe were brought into the homes of people in ancient times, since they thought the berries were magical because they appeared in winter when most other plants died.

Christmas trees were thought by the Vikings to contain the secret of eternal life because the trees kept their leaves in winter. They used to bring them into their homes and hoped for good luck. Christmas trees did not become popular in England until the nineteenth century when Prince Albert, Queen Victoria's husband, was sent one as a present from Norway.

Christingle services can be held during Advent or Christmas. Here, an orange is decorated with a candle, a red tape, and four sticks with fruit on. The orange is the world, the candle is Jesus the light of the world, the red tape is the blood of Jesus, and the four sticks are the four seasons and the fruits of the earth.

The meaning

Christians believe that God came to people in a special way at Christmas. He showed his love for people through the life of Jesus, showed that he is with people and that good is stronger than evil. The birth of Jesus is seen by Christians as a turning point for the world and a hope for a new beginning where nations can live together in peace. This is up to each person, though, and will not happen magically, but Christmas reminds Christians of this goal, this ideal. To sum up this message, Matthew quoted from another Old Testament prophecy:

> The people living in darkness
>   Have seen a great light;
> on those living in the land of the shadow of
>   death
>   a light has dawned.
> *Matthew 4:16*

One carol speaks of the birth of Jesus like this: 'The hopes and fears of all the years are met in thee tonight.'

Christmas makes Christians think of peace. In

▲ **Football in No Man's Land, Christmas, 1914.**

the First World War, in 1914, the fighting stopped in the trenches on Christmas Day and the troops played football with each other and exchanged food and drink.

Most Christians do feel that the events in the Christmas story actually happened. Some do not, though. They believe that Jesus was born, and that God was with him in a special way, but they think the Christmas story is a collection of symbolic stories with a meaning. They think it is a myth. By 'myth' they do not mean that it is not true in any way. They mean that it is not literally true, but has a true *message* or meaning:

■ The Christmas stories are only in *two* of the Gospels (Matthew and Luke), and are not mentioned anywhere else in the New Testament. Mark's Gospel, written earlier, does not mention the story.

■ There were many stories of people being born in a miraculous way in the Greek and Roman world. The great philosopher Plato (fourth century BCE), for example, was said to have been born before his father had had sex with his mother. The god Apollo had made her pregnant. If the Christians wanted to show that Jesus was special, in such a culture, it was natural to invent a story of his miraculous birth. They were not lying: it was a poetic way of saying that God was with him in a special way. He was an outstanding person – Christians believe, the most outstanding person.

■ The prophecy in Isaiah 7:14 can also be translated, 'a *young woman* who is pregnant will have a son ...' It need not imply a **virgin birth**.

Other Christians would argue as follows:

■ It is true that only two Gospels mention the story of the miraculous birth. Yet, two do have the story, and though some details are different, the same core events are told. It is possible that this was not known about until later because Mary kept it a secret. (It would have been very personal.)

■ The story of the birth of Jesus is similar to Greek and Roman stories in some ways, but is different from them in others. In the Greek stories a god usually had sex with a woman, and sometimes even raped her. On the contrary, the Christmas story says a miracle was performed in her womb.

■ Isaiah 7:14 can be translated 'young woman' or 'virgin'. The meaning is open. The Gospel writers certainly took it to mean 'virgin'.

However, all Christians agree that the manner of Jesus' birth is not as important as who he was and what he did. Christians can enjoy the message of Christmas whether they treat its story as symbolic or factual.

TASK BOX

a How was the idea of a virgin birth of Jesus similar to and yet different from pagan ideas of the birth of gods and heroes?
b Why do some people think the virgin birth story is symbolic?
c Why do many Christians continue to believe that many parts of the story are based upon facts?

EPIPHANY

The story

Matthew has the story of the wise men bringing gifts to the baby Jesus (Matthew 2:1–12). He does not say how many men there were, but people have assumed that there were three of them because they brought three gifts (gold, frankincense and myrrh). It is a much later tradition that calls them kings. The word used to describe them in Greek is *magoi*, meaning magicians, astrologers or wise men. They followed a star from the East to Bethlehem. (This event is celebrated by some Churches on 6 January and is known as the Epiphany.)

The celebrations

Churches will use white or gold, and the figures of the wise men will be placed in the crib. Incense might also be used in the service.

The meaning

'Epiphany' means 'showing forth' or 'the appearance'. Jesus revealed his glory to the wise men. The baby in the manger was God become man.

TEST YOURSELF

1 What does Epiphany mean?
2 What event does this recall?
3 What three gifts were bought?
4 Who were the magi (*magoi*)?

LENT, HOLY WEEK AND EASTER

KEY QUESTION

What happened during the last week of Jesus' life, and how are these events remembered today?

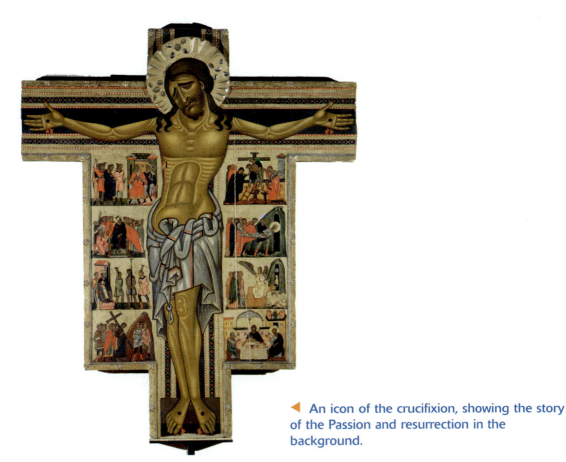

◀ **An icon of the crucifixion, showing the story of the Passion and resurrection in the background.**

The story

The oldest festival that Christians celebrate is that of Easter. It remembers the story of Christ's resurrection. Lent and **Holy Week** build up to this.

The story of the arrest, trial and execution of Jesus takes up most of the space in each of the Gospels. Six out of the 16 chapters in Mark describe the events at the end of Jesus' life. His arrest, trial and crucifixion are known as the Passion. The outline of events is as follows:

1 Jesus went to pray in the Garden of Gethsemane with his disciples on the night of his arrest.
2 Judas betrayed his whereabouts to the Jewish authorities, and led a group of guards to Gethsemane to arrest him.
3 Jesus was taken to the High Priest's house where he was questioned all night. It was in the courtyard here that Peter denied he had ever known his master.
4 The Jewish leaders took Jesus before Pilate, the Roman governor, early in the morning.
5 Pilate questioned him, but found him to be a harmless preacher. He offered to let Jesus go free, but the Jewish leaders threatened to report him to Caesar.
6 Pilate had Jesus whipped, thinking that would satisfy them. He offered to set one of two prisoners free: Jesus, or a revolutionary called Barabbas. The people chose Barabbas.
7 Jesus was forced to carry his own cross, but he fell under the weight of it, and Simon of Cyrene had to help him.
8 Jesus was crucified between two thieves on a hill called Golgotha, just outside Jerusalem. He died after six hours.

Jesus was buried in a tomb that had been donated to the disciples by a rich merchant, Joseph of Arimathea. He was a sympathiser, or maybe a disciple himself. The tomb was cut out of rock in a garden nearby.

Normally, a body would be cleaned and covered with spices to help to preserve it. The Gospels say that Jesus was placed in a burial shroud and put in the tomb quickly because it was Friday evening and the Jewish Sabbath was approaching, when Jews were not allowed to work. The tomb would have been sealed by rolling a huge stone in front of the entrance. This would deter any grave robbers.

Some of the women came to the tomb early on Sunday morning (after the Jewish Sabbath) to prepare Jesus' body properly with the right spices. They found that the stone had been rolled away and that the tomb was empty. A young man in white, according to one Gospel, or an angel according to another, told them that Jesus had risen.

 'Don't be alarmed,' he said. 'You are looking for Jesus the Nazarene, who was crucified. He has risen! He is not here. See the place where they laid him. But go, tell his disciples and Peter, "He is going ahead of you into Galilee. There you will see him, just as he told you."'

Mark 16:6–7

Mark ends there rather suddenly. Some people think there was originally more to his Gospel, but the ending was lost as it was copied and handed down. The other Gospels carry on the story:

1 The women tell the disciples, and they think the women have gone mad.
2 Peter goes to the tomb to check, and finds it empty.
3 Jesus appears to the disciples several times, either all together or in small groups.
4 They all return to Jerusalem and meet behind locked doors for fear of the Romans.
5 Later, they find the courage to carry on preaching.

John has an account of an appearance to all the disciples at once: 'Jesus came and stood among them and said, "Peace be with you!" After he said this, he showed them his hands and side. The dis-ciples were overjoyed when they saw the Lord' (John 20:19–20).

Luke (24:13–35) has a story of an appearance to two disciples walking along the road from Jerusalem to Emmaus. They did not recognise him at first, but realised who it was when he shared some bread with them. Then he vanished. They said afterwards that their hearts had felt as though they had burned within them as he talked with them.

So the resurrection story involves three aspects: (1) the empty tomb, (2) appearances of the risen Christ, (3) the revived faith of the disciples, many of whom had given up. Instead, they found new life and courage.

TEST YOURSELF

1 How many chapters of Mark concern the Passion story?
2 What happened in the Garden of Gethsemane?
3 Who was Pilate and what did he do?
4 What did Simon of Cyrene do?
5 Who went to the empty tomb?

The celebrations

▲ An Easter Vigil.

The date of Easter varies each year because it is based on the Jewish calendar, which follows the cycle of the moon, not the sun, as in our calendar.

A New Approach – Christianity

LENT

Anglican, Roman Catholic and Orthodox Christians keep a period of 40 days before Easter, known as Lent. This period recalls the time Jesus spent in the desert being tempted by the Devil. It used to be a time of fasting, with only certain foods being eaten (meat, dairy produce and alcohol were not eaten, as is still the case in the Orthodox Churches). Shrove Tuesday is a leftover of this, when sweet pancakes are made. This was a final feast before Lent began the following day. Lent begins on Ash Wednesday and is a period of reflection and preparation. A special Eucharist is held on Ash Wednesday, and the sign of the cross is made upon the foreheads of worshippers with ashes. It is to show humility.

Many Christians today give up something for Lent (e.g. sweets, or sugar in drinks) or might spend more time in prayer or the study of the Bible. It is a time of reflection and spiritual preparation as people think about their lives and prepare for Easter, when they are to celebrate the most important events in their faith. Purple is used in the church, a traditional colour for sorrow and mourning in the ancient world, and flowers are removed. The churches are as bare as possible, as Lent is a penitential season.

HOLY WEEK

Palm Sunday

Holy Week starts on Palm Sunday and ends on Holy Saturday, recalling the events of the last week of Jesus' life. The story of Jesus riding into Jerusalem on a donkey is remembered on **Palm Sunday** (read Mark 11:1–10). Small crosses made from palm leaves are given out in churches and are held by worshippers during the service. Some churches will have a procession around the church or the local area. In Israel, Christians carry palm leaves and large wooden crosses from Bethphage to Jerusalem, trying to follow the route Jesus would have taken himself. The Ethiopian Orthodox Church uses decorative palms for Palm Sunday. These might be a ring of woven palm leaves worn around the finger, or a crown around the head.

Meaning of Palm Sunday

The story of Jesus riding into Jerusalem is full of

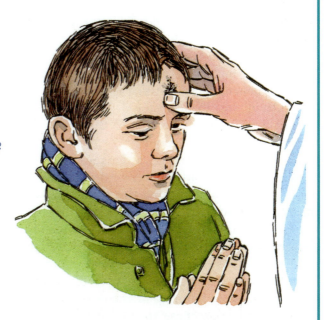

TASK BOX

'Remember that you are dust and to dust you shall return. Turn to Christ and believe the Gospel.'
Saying at the placing of ash on the forehead.

a Why do you think ashes are used on Ash Wednesday?
b What is meant by the saying about being dust?

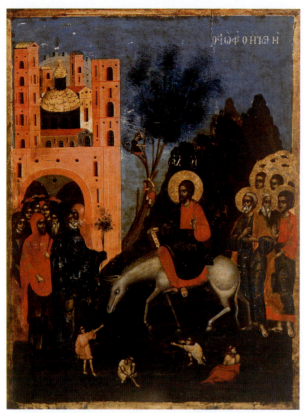

▲ An icon of Jesus riding into Jerusalem on a donkey, where he was cheered as the coming Messiah.

▲ An icon of the Resurrection and descent into Hell, remembered on Easter Sunday. (See page 65.)

meanings hidden from people today unless they are explained. The people were cheering Jesus as the coming Messiah, and many were expecting a warrior Messiah who would drive the Romans out. The palm branches they waved were signs of victory, and they used to be waved after a battle was won, when people rejoiced in the streets. The people thought that the 'kingdom of King David' was to be restored. David was an ancient Jewish king who united the tribes of Israel into a mighty kingdom.

Yet Jesus came riding on a donkey. It is not exactly the way a warrior would ride to victory. Some people have compared this to the idea of the Prime Minister arriving on a scooter rather than in a Jaguar! Perhaps Jesus was deliberately showing that he was not the kind of Messiah most people were expecting: he was a humble man of peace. A verse in the Old Testament could be taken as referring to the arrival of the Messiah, and Jesus chose to fulfil it because it suited his purposes:

Rejoice greatly, O Daughter of Zion!
    Shout, Daughter of Jerusalem!
See, your king comes to you,
    righteous and having salvation,
    gentle and riding on a donkey,
    on a colt, the foal of a donkey.
Zechariah 9:9

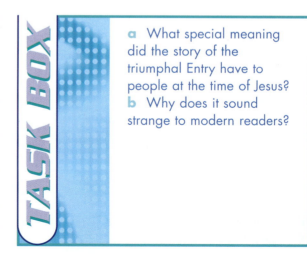

TASK BOX

a What special meaning did the story of the triumphal Entry have to people at the time of Jesus?
b Why does it sound strange to modern readers?

A New Approach – Christianity

Maundy Thursday

Maundy Thursday is the next special day in Holy Week. The name comes from a Latin word *mandatum*, meaning 'commandment', and it refers to the commandment to love one another that Jesus gave on the night of the Last Supper, before he was arrested.

Many churches include a foot-washing ceremony as a part of the Eucharist on this day. Some people sit at the front of the church and have their feet washed by the priest. This is because Jesus did this to the disciples in the upper room where they ate the Last Supper:

When he had finished washing their feet, he put on his clothes and returned to his place. 'Do you understand what I have done for you?' He asked them. 'You call me "Teacher" and "Lord", and rightly so, for that is what I am. Now that I, your Lord and Teacher, have washed your feet, you also should wash one another's feet. I have set you an example that you should do as I have done for you.'
John 13:12–15

Meaning of Maundy Thursday

Foot-washing was common in the East where the people walked in sandals on dry, dusty roads. It was usually the job of the servants to wash the feet of guests. Jesus was saying that Christians should love and serve one another.

Good Friday

The crucifixion of Jesus is remembered on **Good Friday**. This is a serious and sombre occasion.

Roman Catholic, Orthodox and some Anglican churches are stripped of all colourful decorations, crosses, candles and hangings. This is to remind the worshippers of the fact that Jesus felt deserted and desolate on the cross. The story of the **Passion** is read, and, in some churches, the

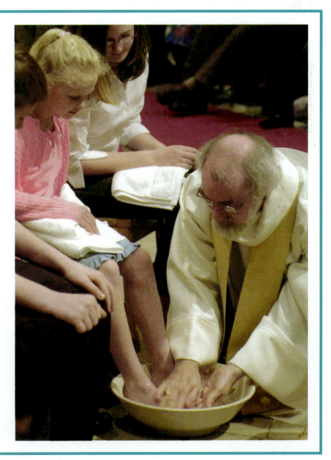

TASK BOX

a Why is the Archbishop of Canterbury washing people's feet?
b When would this have taken place?
c Why did Jesus do this?

priest will unveil a crucifix and say, 'This is the wood of the cross on which the Saviour of the world died.' The people will then walk up to the altar to kiss the feet of the carved Christ as a mark of respect.

Free Churches do not have the same ritual, but they have a special service where the Passion story is read, and thanks are given because Jesus went to the cross to save humanity from their sins.

Meaning of Good Friday

All Churches teach that the death of Jesus saved the world somehow, although they have different ways of explaining that. Perhaps the easiest way is by thinking of the cross as a token of the love of God present in Christ: he was prepared to be rejected and he suffered, but he still forgives people. As a popular Easter hymn says, 'There is a green hill far away, / without a city wall, / where the dear Lord was crucified, / who

died to save us all.' The day is 'Good Friday' rather than 'Bad Friday' because Christians believe that our sins were forgiven then.

Easter Vigil

Roman Catholic, Orthodox and some Anglican churches keep an Easter **Vigil** on the Saturday evening. The congregation gather outside the church, where a bonfire is burning. A large candle is brought out, called the Paschal Candle. It has a cross on it and the Greek letters alpha and omega. The priest places five grains of incense on it, in memory of the five wounds Jesus received on the cross (both wrists, both feet and a spear wound in his side). The candle is then lit and the priest leads a procession into the church, holding the candle up high, and saying, 'Christ our Light'. The people reply, 'Thanks be to God!' They then carry small candles lit from the Paschal Candle and hold them during the Eucharist.

TASK BOX

a Why are these people honouring the cross?
b When would this happen?
c Why is 'Good Friday' so called?
d What does a priest say when a cross is unveiled in the church service on Good Friday?

The vigil is in preparation for the celebration of the resurrection the next day. If Good Friday seems to be about the victory of darkness, then the ceremony of the light symbolises the victory of Jesus over death.

TASK BOX

a Why does light symbolise the risen Christ?
b What does a blazing bonfire suggest?

Easter Sunday

This is the day of the resurrection, the third day after Jesus died. Anglican, Roman Catholic and Orthodox churches are full of decoration again with the priest in white robes, flowers on the altar and candles burning. Songs of victory are sung in all churches, such as, 'Thine be the glory, / risen conquering Son. / Endless is the victory / thou over death has won ...'

The story of the empty tomb and the appearances of the risen Jesus will be read out.

Some customs

Eating hot-cross buns began as a way of celebrating the end of Lent. The cross design, of course, remembers the death of Jesus.

The Easter egg is a symbol of new life. In Orthodox churches, hard-boiled eggs are coloured red to suggest blood, and are cracked open on Easter Day to celebrate the resurrection when Jesus burst free from the tomb.

The Easter egg might also be linked with ancient religion and the celebration of spring, when new life comes. The name 'Easter' comes from the old Saxon spring goddess, Eostre. The early Christians in Britain probably thought springtime was an appropriate time to remember the death and resurrection of Christ because it is a season of hope and new life.

The Ethiopian Orthodox Church calls Easter *Fassika*. Tall candles (*twaf*) are sold outside churches, being thin threads of cotton bound with wax. The churches are ablaze with light for the service celebrating the resurrection. People wear white robes (*yabesha libs*) and the prayers go on from 8 p.m. until 3 a.m. The families will celebrate by sharing a special meal afterwards, *injera*, a mutton stew eaten with pancakes and cottage cheese.

▲ A priest outside an Ethiopian church.

TEST YOURSELF

1 What colour tends to be used in churches at Easter?
2 Why do Christians have Easter eggs?
3 How do Orthodox Christians decorate their eggs?
4 What do Ethiopian Christians call Easter, and what do they all carry during the service?

The disciples' conviction that they had seen the risen Christ, their permanent relocation to Jerusalem, their principled inclusion of Gentiles as Gentiles – all these are historical bedrock, facts known past doubting about the earliest community after Jesus' death ...

Paula Fredriksen, **Jesus of Nazareth, King of the Jews**

This scholar does not think we can prove, beyond all doubt, that Jesus rose again. What does she think we can prove, though?

The meaning of Easter

The story of Jesus' passion and resurrection is a movement from tears to joy, and touches Christians deeply when they hear it. It is about the struggle between good and evil, or light and darkness, and the final victory of good. It is about an innocent teacher of peace being persecuted by an oppressive government and being put to death, and yet his message of love goes on. Even more, for the Christian, it is the story of how God showed that he was involved in human struggles and suffering, and of how God promises life after death.

GOING DEEPER

The Passion narrative

New Testament scholars think that the earliest continuous story told about Jesus was the Passion. It takes up a large proportion of space in each of the Gospels, and might have been the first narrative about Jesus to have been written down. The Gospel writers adapted earlier versions of the story to fit in with their Gospels. (Despite a few small differences they all tell the same story.)

The reason for telling the Passion story as a connected story so early may have been twofold:

- To use it in the celebration of the Eucharist, remembering the details of the Last Supper.
- To use it to show both Jews and Romans that Jesus had not really been a criminal.

Why was Jesus killed? Crucifixion was a criminal's death. When the Romans heard that the Christians followed a crucified master, they would have suspected them of antisocial behaviour. Christians believe Jesus was a preacher of peace and love, challenging people to let the Kingdom of God enter their hearts. Why was he put to death? A possible answer is that the Jewish authorities were frightened that he might cause an uprising of the people because he was so popular (as can be seen in the story of the entry into Jerusalem). The Romans would then step in and many people might lose their lives. If the Jews handed him over to the Romans, and he was executed, then people would think he was a failure and stop following him.

Although Pilate found Jesus to be harmless in himself, the Romans would have been glad to have any potential troublemaker out of the way. John's Gospel suggests that the Romans were involved in the plot to have Jesus killed, because a Roman cohort (about 480 men) accompanied the Jewish Temple guards to the Garden of Gethsemane to arrest Jesus (John 18:3).

Why did Judas betray Jesus?

It has often puzzled people why Judas, one of the Twelve, should have betrayed his master. The usual explanation given is that he did it for the money: he was paid 30 silver coins by the Temple authorities. But this was not a large amount: it was the traditional price paid for the loss of a slave. Furthermore, Judas was filled with guilt and committed suicide after Jesus' death. (Matthew 27:5 says he hanged himself; Acts 1:18 suggests he fell on a sword.) It is therefore hard to imagine that he was only in it for the money.

It is possible that Judas misunderstood Jesus. He might have really believed that Jesus was going to drive the Romans out, either by giving the people a sign to rise up in revolt or by bringing God's supernatural Kingdom crashing in. He might also have feared that the people were losing faith in Jesus after his entry into Jerusalem – many people would have been waiting for his signal then, but nothing happened. Judas might therefore have arranged the arrest in order to corner Jesus and force his hand; yet this backfired upon him and Judas could not live with himself when he realised he had betrayed an innocent man of peace.

Facts and symbols

Some people think that the style of writing the gospel writers used should not be taken as straightforward reporting of facts. The gospel writers are always trying to interpret what Jesus said and did; and perhaps sometimes they add details to the story that are symbolic.

This might be seen in some of the details of the story of the death of Jesus. Mark says that at noon the whole country was covered in darkness, and three hours later Jesus died. Mark then adds that the curtain hanging in the Temple was torn in two, from top to bottom.

The darkness may have been some form of eclipse, but it could be a symbolic point: the time when Jesus was dying was a time of spiritual darkness; it seemed like a victory of evil over good.

The curtain in the Temple covered the entrance to the most holy part of it, the Holy of Holies, where only the High Priest could go, where it was believed he was in the presence of God. There is no evidence from any Jewish writings of anything happening to the curtain. Mark may have been writing symbolically: Jesus had died to bring God to all the earth; he could not be contained in a Temple any more – it was 'torn open'.

TASK BOX

a Why was the Passion story written down early on?

b Give two ideas to explain why Judas might have betrayed Jesus.

c What happened to the curtain in the Temple? What was the significance of this?

d How is the symbol of darkness used in the Passion narrative? Might there be any facts behind this?

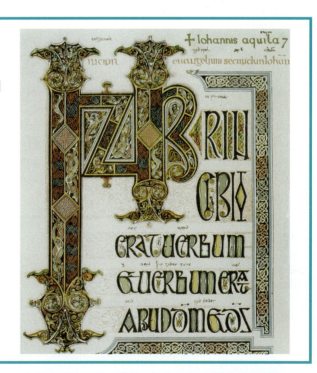

▶ The title page of *St John's Gospel* from the *Lindisfarne Gospels*.

The resurrection: what happened?

Most Christians believe the stories of the resurrection in the Gospels, but some doubt the story of the empty tomb.

- They think the story of the empty tomb was a detail added later to make the resurrection sound more dramatic.
- They point out that the earliest mention of the resurrection story (in Paul's first letter to the Corinthians 15:3–7, written before the Gospels) does not mention the empty tomb at all. It just says that Jesus was raised and appeared to Peter, the rest of the Twelve, and to over 500 disciples, then to James, and finally to Paul.
- They feel that the empty tomb story makes the resurrection sound too physical: Jesus was not just a dead body come back to life, but a transformed spirit.

Traditional believers point out that they do not believe that Jesus was just a dead man come back to life, either.

- He was transformed and was alive in a new way, but his physical body was transformed, too. The body was not left to rot.
- The stories of the appearances of Jesus show he was different; sometimes he was not recognised at first, and sometimes he appeared and disappeared suddenly. See, for example, Luke 24:13–32 and John 20:19–21.
- If the empty tomb story was made up, it is hard to see why the women were made out to be the first witnesses, as in Jewish society the word of a woman was not valid in a court of law. Also, all four Gospels have a version of the empty tomb story.

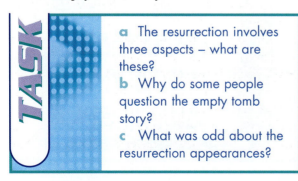

TASK

a The resurrection involves three aspects – what are these?
b Why do some people question the empty tomb story?
c What was odd about the resurrection appearances?

PENTECOST

KEY QUESTION
What is remembered at Pentecost?

The story

Pentecost celebrates the reawakening of faith in the disciples after the resurrection. This reawakening, and sense of renewed courage, is seen as a result of the gift of the Holy Spirit.

The fullest account of it in the New Testament is in Acts 2:1–42. The disciples were gathered together in prayer, waiting for the coming of the Holy Spirit, as Jesus had told them to: 'Suddenly a sound like the blowing of a violent wind came from heaven and filled the whole house where they were sitting. They saw what seemed to be tongues of fire that separated and came to rest on each of them. All of them were filled with the Holy Spirit and began to speak in other tongues as the Spirit enabled them' (Acts 2:2–4).

When people came to listen, Peter explained what had happened by quoting an Old Testament passage (from Joel 2:28): 'In the last days, God says, "I will pour out my Spirit on all people"' (Acts 2:17). Then Peter went on to explain: 'God has raised this Jesus to life, and we are all witnesses of the fact. Exalted to the right hand of God, he has received from the Father the promised Holy Spirit and has poured out what you now see and hear' (Acts 2:32–3).

This is said in Acts to have happened 50 days after the crucifixion, on the day of the Jewish feast of Pentecost, which celebrated the giving of the Law to Moses. John's Gospel, however, gives a different version of the events, where the gift of the Holy Spirit is given to the disciples in the upper room when they first see the risen Christ (20:22). There are no tongues of fire or roaring wind in this version. Both accounts agree that the gift of the Holy Spirit was given, though.

El Greco's interpretation of Pentecost.

The celebrations

The main celebration is on Pentecost Sunday. Special reference is made to the gift of the Holy Spirit during the service in church, and the story from Acts is read out.

Churches are decorated in red for the fire of the Spirit. Sometimes Christians will be confirmed in the faith at this time, when a bishop lays his hands on their heads and prays for the Spirit to come into their lives (see p107).

During Pentecost some churches take part in walks of witness through a town – Christians will carry banners with simple messages or texts from the Scriptures on them. Their walk ends with a short service in a church or in the open air. The walk recalls the boldness of the disciples when they first went out preaching.

The meaning

What may have happened is that the disciples were downhearted and confused after the crucifixion, but their energy and faith revived when they came to believe that Jesus had risen from the dead. This renewal was possibly a gradual process until they felt that God was alive within them in a new, fresh way. So John has the coming of the life-giving Spirit at the same time as the first sight of the risen Christ; and the writer of Acts has the full revival coming later when things had sunk in more.

The wind and fire in the Acts story may be symbols. The writer probably does not mean his readers to think that there were physical wind and fire there. Instead it is poetry – a way of describing the disciples' revival of faith.

The Holy Spirit is often pictured as wind or fire in the Bible. Wind suggests power, an invisible force that cannot be controlled. Fire suggests the warmth of love or joy, and the light of knowledge and purity. The Acts passage is using this picture-language to show that the lives of the disciples were being shaken up; their fears disappeared (burned away) and they saw with the inner eye of faith that Christ was alive (the light of knowledge).

The result of the gift of the Spirit was that the disciples went out fearlessly, teaching the

TEST YOURSELF

A B C

1 What does the *Jewish* festival of Pentecost remember?

2 What does the *Christian* festival of Pentecost remember?

3 What happened involving wind, fire and other languages?

message of Jesus, even when their lives were threatened (read Acts 4:18–22, for example).

The 'other languages' (Acts 2:4) spoken by the disciples are understood by a number of Christians today as the gift of speaking in tongues (see p84). They feel that this gift is still carrying on. The languages should not be understood as a miracle that gave the apostles the ability to speak any language so that they could preach the Gospel to all nations without learning anything new. This would be like a God-given translator device that we see in science fiction adventures! That is not the inten-

tion of the story. The apostles prayed and praised in a new prayer language that bubbled up from their hearts. Some overheard their languages represented.

Behind the story is a memory of the Tower of Babel (Genesis 11) when all the earth spoke a single language. Part of the judgement upon their pride was that they were scattered and then had different languages. At Pentecost there was a healing, a bringing together again under the blessing of God. Believers are given new languages, moved by the Spirit as a gift from God.

TASK BOX

a Why is the wind a symbol of the Holy Spirit?

b What do people think the wind and flames symbolise in the Acts story?

c The gift of tongues to the apostles is all about bringing the nations back to God – why?

d Think about how to celebrate life. This can be done in a non-religious way. You can read a poem, play a piece of music, show a video clip, bring a symbolic object (flowers, a piece of crystal, or something beautiful), use a bowl of water, share a cup of mineral water. Try a short meditation, imagining a scene in a colourful garden with a clear fountain and birds singing. By using objects and actions, by using words and music, by listening and stillness, you are using human means of celebration, all of which can be found in festivals.

e Choose one Christian festival and list all the elements of a celebration, as above, that can be found there.

Assignment

1 Describe events during Holy Week. [8]

2 Explain how and why the keeping of Lent may affect the life of a Christian. [7]

3 'The example set by Jesus is impossible to follow, so people shouldn't even try to follow.' Do you agree? Give reasons for your answer, showing that you have considered other points of view. [5]

4 When is Advent? [2]

5 Describe why Christmas is seen as a festival of light, and how light is used in the celebrations. [6]

6 Explain why the idea of having Christmas cribs first came about. [8]

7 'Christmas is really about being selfish and greedy, and is a good excuse for a party.' Do you agree? Show how the meaning of the Christmas story might give rise to a different point of view. [4]

WEBLINKS

A site about different Christmas customs is at

🕷 www.soon.org.uk/country/christmas.htm

A site about the Easter story can be found at

🕷 www.topmarks.co.uk/christianity/easter/easter.htm

REMEMBER

▶ We all need to remember important events and to celebrate them.

▶ Christians celebrate the birth of Jesus, his death and resurrection and the coming of the Holy Spirit.

▶ Some Christians take many details in the stories as symbolic, some take them all as literally true and some as a mixture of act and symbol.

KEY WORDS

Assumption – the belief that Mary was taken into heaven, body and soul.

Bishop – an overseer in the Church.

Cardinal – a senior Roman Catholic Bishop.

Catholic – literally 'worldwide'.

Charismatic – a believer open to the renewal of the Holy Spirit.

Church – an assembly of Christian worshippers.

Counter-Reformation – a Roman Catholic movement that sought to reform the Church without becoming Protestant.

Denomination – one type of Church, or group of believers.

Diocese – a group of churches under a bishop.

Ecumenism – the Churches working together for unity.

Ekklesia – Greek word for 'assembly' or 'church'.

Elder – an early name for a church leader, later called a 'priest'.

Heresy – splitting away from the Church and holding unorthodox teaching.

Inquisition – a movement that sought to stamp out heresy in the medieval Roman Catholic Church.

Pope – the Bishop of Rome.

Protestant – originally, a protestor against the power of the Pope.

Purgatory – a preparation for heaven.

Reformation – a movement that sought to change the medieval Church.

Sacrament – an action that conveys a spiritual blessing.

KEY QUESTION

What is meant by the 'Church'?

THE CHURCH

The Greek word **ekklesia** was used for the **Church** in the New Testament. It means an assembly of people, a believing community. The people who make up the Church are each trying to carry on the work of Jesus in some way in response to his teaching, and so the New Testament calls the Church the Body of Christ (i.e. a group of people trying to follow Christ on earth, with his Spirit within them).

The Church is described in the Nicene Creed as being *one, holy, catholic* and *apostolic*.

Catholic does not just mean Roman Catholic, but 'worldwide'. Apostolic means it is based on the teachings of the apostles, which were handed down in the New Testament. There are many different **denominations** or types of Church that

have been formed over the ages as people have had different ideas about what to believe and how to worship, but at heart they are all part of the same faith.

All of you are Christ's body, and each one is a part of it.

1 Corinthians 12:27
(Good News Bible)

a What is St Paul trying to say about the Church, the assembly of Christian believers?

b How would this make people from very different backgrounds feel?

c Is this the way people generally use the term Church today?

TASK BOX

The Christian Church today is divided into a number of different groups or denominations, but when Christianity first began there was only one Church. Local groups were led by elders. A senior **elder** was sometimes called an overseer. (The names for these officials in the Greek language was *presbyter* and *episkopos*). These people were later known as priests and **bishops**. In the large cities there were senior bishops, and the bishop of Rome was given special respect. Other senior bishops were in the ancient cities of Alexandria, Jerusalem, Constantinople and Antioch.

After a while, however, various groups started separating from the main Church. A major split came in the eleventh century when the Western and Eastern sections of the Church separated from each other. Some Eastern churches had separated earlier in the fifth century CE, over different ways of understanding Jesus. The Eastern churches became known as the Orthodox churches.

Five hundred years after the East/West split there was a major split in the Western Church. A movement known as the **Reformation** questioned many of the traditional teachings. These Reformed churches, also known as **Protestant** churches, would no longer accept the Pope (the bishop of Rome) as leader. Some of them kept bishops but some did not, looking mainly to the Bible for their guidance. The term Protestant came from the word protest. Protestants were *protesting* against the corruptions of the medieval Church.

Protestant churches also divided and disagreed, spawning many offshoots such as the Baptist Church and the Methodist Church.

TEST YOURSELF

1 When did the Eastern churches separate from Rome?
2 What was the Reformation?
3 Who were the Protestants?
4 Who is the Pope?

TASK BOX

a This is the typical costume for a bishop with mitre and staff. This developed slowly. The early Church bishops did not have any distinctive dress. They just looked like ordinary people who were leaders. How would you dress bishops today if you had the chance of designing their clothes?

b Say why you would dress a modern bishop in the way you have described above.

c Find out what different churches are in your area. Look these up in the Yellow Pages or town directory. Ask each person to phone one number and to try to speak to the minister or priest. Ask them what they do to try to work with the other churches.

d Draw a map of the area and display this on the wall. Mark on it the different churches consulted and write a few sentences saying what they are doing to work together, to be ecumenical.

THE ROMAN CATHOLIC CHURCH

The Roman Catholic Church has the **Pope** as its leader (from Latin *papa*, meaning father). A number of bishops used to be given this title out of respect, but it became reserved for the Bishop of Rome. The Pope is the Bishop of Rome, and hence the 'Roman' part of the name. The word catholic means worldwide and all the churches in the world in union with the Pope are Roman Catholic churches. About half of all the Christians in the world are Roman Catholics.

Roman Catholics believe that Jesus made Peter the leader of the Church after his death and that Peter eventually took charge of the Church in Rome, where he was martyred for the faith. His bones lie beneath St Peter's Church in the Vatican. Therefore the bishops of Rome are seen as his successors. The Pope lives in the Vatican, an independent state in Rome. The chief bishops help to advise him and are called **cardinals**. Each local area has a bishop to look after it, with parish priests under him. These areas are called **dioceses**.

> Jesus replied, 'Blessed are you, Simon son of Jonah ... And I tell you that you are Peter, and on this rock I will build my church, and the gates of Hades will not overcome it.'
>
> *Matthew 16:17–18*

Roman Catholics believe that the Pope is infallible when he speaks about issues regarding faith or morals. He has to follow the tradition of the Church and to have a large consent of the faithful for what he pronounces.

This question of authority is the main difference between Roman Catholics and other Christians.

Priests are usually celibate (remaining single and abstaining from sexual relationships). Ministers of other Churches can usually marry.

▲ Cardinal Cormac Murphy-O'Connor (left) with the Archbishop of Canterbury and a US bishop in 2003.

A New Approach – Christianity

A cluster of ceremonies and doctrines developed, which the Reformers rejected in the sixteenth century:

- the cult of the saints and the Virgin Mary
- the belief in transubstantiation in the Mass
- the belief in purgatory and prayer for the dead
- the seven sacraments.

TEST YOURSELF

1 What does 'Roman Catholic' mean?
2 What do Roman Catholics believe about the Pope?
3 What is celibacy?

KEY QUESTION

What are the main differences between Roman Catholics and other Christians?

The saints and Mary

Outstanding Christians, especially the martyrs, were commemorated year by year by the early Christians. Gradually, it became the custom to ask for their prayers, rather as a believer might ask someone to pray for them on earth. It was thought that the saints were in glory, and closer to God, and so their prayers were more powerful. This was especially true of the Virgin Mary, who, as the mother of Jesus, was given special honour. Roman Catholics believe she was conceived without the effects of original sin (see p31). This is known as her immaculate conception. They also believe she was taken into heaven, body and soul at the point of her death. This is known as the **Assumption**.

Protestant Christians are wary of the cult of the saints for they fear this distracts people from praying through Jesus alone. Similarly, too much honour of Mary slips into worship of her, in their view. Doctrines such as the immaculate conception and the Assumption are not in the Bible.

Transubstantiation

Roman Catholics developed a particular theory of how Jesus was present in the Eucharist and hold this as a binding doctrine for the Church. They feel this is the truest understanding of what happens to the bread and wine when they are consecrated by a priest.

The invisible substance is that of the body and blood of Jesus, but the physical, visible aspects are those of bread and wine. Theologians referred to these as 'the accidents'. Protestant believers reject this theory, believing that Jesus gives himself along with the bread and wine but that there is not such a change.

Purgatory and prayer for the dead

By the Middle Ages, **purgatory** had become an intermediate place between heaven and hell. It was a place of purification and correction for souls who would ultimately be saved and enter heaven. These souls could do nothing for themselves, but the prayers of those on earth could aid them, and special observances and offerings could release them from their suffering all the quicker. These methods of quick release were called indulgences, and some of these could even be bought.

Prayer for the dead was an early Christian practice, commending them to God's care and mercy, but the whole medieval system was nowhere in evidence. Likewise, the Scriptures speak about being confronted by the holy fire of God's love after death, but there is no description of an intermediate place. It was like an initial encounter with God before entering heaven.

> For no-one can lay any foundation other than the one already laid, which is Jesus Christ. If any man builds on this foundation using gold, silver, costly stones, wood, hay or straw, his work will be shown for what it is, because the Day will bring it to light. It will be revealed with fire, and the fire will test the quality of each man's work.
>
> *1 Corinthians 3:11–13*

Roman Catholics still believe in purgatory and prayer for the dead, but not in the old medieval manner: there is a preparation to enter heaven and prayers can aid the departed.

Seven sacraments

The Roman Catholic Church gradually accepted seven rituals as sacraments. A **sacrament** is an action that conveys a spiritual blessing. There is an inner and an outer meaning. These are outward actions that have an inner, invisible spiritual effect. The seven were:

- Baptism
- Eucharist
- Confirmation
- Reconciliation (Confession)
- Ordination
- Marriage
- Anointing of the sick.

The Reformers accepted only two as sacraments (Baptism and Eucharist) as these were actually mentioned in the Gospels and were directly from Jesus. In essence, though, a number of the other items were used in their churches. These were seen as deriving from the apostles.

Thus, James teaches about holy oil and prayer for the sick: 'Is any one of you sick? He should call the elders of the church to pray over him and anoint him with oil in the name of the Lord' (James 5:14).

TASK BOX

a Why do some Christians have images of Mary like this icon?
b Why do some other Christians refuse to use objects like these?
c What two doctrines about Mary are not held by some Christians?
d What can all Christians agree upon about Mary?

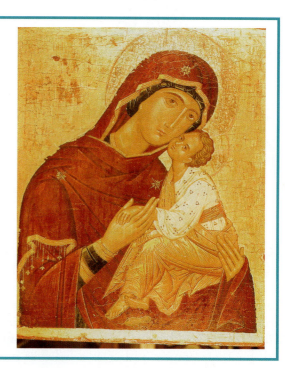

A New Approach – Christianity

In many ways the Reformation was one of the greatest tragedies that ever happened to the Church. Martin Luther never wanted to split the Church, simply to reform it. We no doubt glory in biblical truths that were rediscovered at the Reformation ... but from the Reformation onwards the body of Christ in the world has been torn limb from limb into hundreds of separate pieces ... I have sensed a little of the pain that Christ must always feel when we separate from one another, when in effect we say to him, 'You died to make us one, and we don't care!' Jesus surely weeps for the state of his Body, the Church, on earth today.
David Watson

David Watson was an Evangelical and an Anglican priest. His statement shocked many Protestants who thought he was betraying their cause. From what he said above, do you think they were being fair?

▲ Anointing the sick, one of the seven sacraments.

TEST YOURSELF

1 What is a sacrament?
2 List the seven sacraments of the Roman Catholic Church.
3 What is purgatory?

THE ORTHODOX CHURCHES

KEY QUESTION

Who are the Orthodox Christians?

Orthodox Christians believe that their Church has guarded the right belief since the time of Jesus (orthodox means 'right belief' and 'right worship').

In the fifth and sixth centuries, some churches in the East separated over their understanding of Jesus. The next major split was in 1054. The Eastern Orthodox Church did not agree that the Pope had total authority over them and he excommunicated its members (declared them to be outside the Church). The patriarchs condemned the Pope in return. These condemnations have been lifted only in recent years, and the two Churches are friendly again, though still not united, for they disagree on some matters.

The main reason for the split was the understanding of authority. The Orthodox Church was prepared to respect the Pope as a fellow Patriarch. They would even grant that he was like an elder bishop, whose wisdom on matters would be especially welcomed, but they would not accept that he was the sole leader of the Church on earth.

A further disagreement was over a technical understanding of the Holy Spirit. The Western Church had inserted a phrase in the Nicene

Creed: *filioque* (meaning 'and from the Son'). The Creed says, 'the Holy Spirit, who proceeds from the Father and the Son ...' They believed that the Spirit came not only from the Father, but from the Son as well. The Eastern Church felt that this made the Spirit inferior and the Son too superior. In their view, the Son and the Spirit were sent from the Father to do his work in the world, like his right hand and left hand. This technical difficulty has still not been resolved between the Churches, though the Western Church is saying they never intended to make the Son superior. The Spirit came from the Father uniquely, but through the Son. East and West had developed differently in many ways.

The East also allowed priests to be married and allowed divorce and remarriage. In many other ways they are close to the Roman Catholic Church, having a strong sense of church tradition, elaborate rituals and a belief in the seven sacraments (though some feel there are more!).

▲ **The Serbian Orthodox Patriarch Pavle.**

TEST YOURSELF

1 What does orthodox mean?
2 Who are the Patriarchs?
3 What is the *filioque*?

THE REFORMATION

KEY QUESTION

What caused the Western Church to split in the sixteenth century?

The Western Church was divided about 500 years after the split with the Orthodox. Many of its members felt that things needed changing, or reforming, for the better, and so the split is known as the Reformation. Some of the Church's leaders were political figures who the reformers thought should be more spiritual, and also some priests were uneducated and careless. They did not take their jobs seriously enough.

Furthermore, pardoners were going round selling relics to people, and assuring them that this would cancel out their sins. They claimed the relics were holy objects, such as bits of saints' bones. Most of them were forgeries, though some would have been genuine. It has been said that there were enough pieces of wood from the 'true cross' to build a galleon, and phials of the 'blood of Christ' were often just the blood of an unlucky farmyard goat. Some people even claimed to have feathers from the wings of the archangel Gabriel!

There was also a tendency for some to teach that a sinner had to go and do various good works to earn forgiveness from Christ. This was the very reversal of the gospel message (in which God's grace would meet sinners where they were, and forgive them, with good works following on from this).

Matters came to a head when Johann Tetzel, a Dominican pardoner, arrived in Wittenberg in Germany to collect money for the rebuilding of St Peter's in Rome. He sold indulgences to do this. An indulgence was a document signed by the Pope that granted forgiveness for sins and release from purgatory (the in-between state between heaven and hell). He even had a sales jingle, 'As soon as the coin in the coffer rings, the soul from purgatory springs'! Poor, uneducated people parted with their money thinking that this would release dead relatives from purgatory. A monk called Martin Luther was horrified. He

A New Approach – Christianity

▲ The German Reformer, Martin Luther.

was a professor of the Bible at the university and had been thinking of how the Church had needed reforming for some time. He had been plagued by guilt and fear of hell, and was overzealous in saying prayers and fasting.

Then he rediscovered Paul's teaching about the grace of God that does not have to be earned and he felt a powerful release from guilt by the inner sense of the forgiveness of God. In 1517, he nailed a document that contained 95 theses, or points, for discussion to the cathedral door in Wittenberg. Among them the sale of indulgences was attacked. This was intended for local discussion among his students, but the printing press had been invented by then, and his ideas were spread all over Europe.

Luther was suspected of **heresy** (going against the teaching of the Church) and was summoned to see the Holy Roman Emperor, Charles V, at Worms in 1521. He was ordered to renounce his teachings but refused. He was outlawed but was protected by the German princes who wanted to be independent of their emperor. Luther rejected the Pope as Head of the Church, and

believed that only the Bible should be given such authority to guide Christians.

Luther had started far more than he realised. Other people spread similar ideas and these people became known as Protestants, protesters against the Pope.

The Reformers had pointed out the need for change in the Church, to remove superstition and to rediscover the message of the unconditional love of God that did not have to be earned; but they were intolerant themselves of those who differed from their point of view. Many Roman Catholics agree that their Church did need a reformation, but not the way it happened. They feel that Luther went too far in rejecting the Pope. People were not as ready to listen, though, in those days. The Pope branded Luther as an anti-Christ, and Luther returned the compliment.

At the time, there were many Roman Catholics, such as Ignatius Loyola, who were determined to reform their Church from within. Loyola was a soldier who had to rest for a while in 1521 because of a leg wound. All he could find to read were a Bible and some saints' lives. He was converted to a more committed faith, and devised a set of spiritual exercises upon his recovery. These were a series of disciplined meditations on the life of Christ and on his own personal failings. He gathered some followers, and founded the Society of Jesus (the Jesuits) in 1540. Such people led a movement in the Roman Church known as the **Counter-Reformation** – to stop the spread of Protestant ideas by improving the Roman Catholic Church from within.

TEST YOURSELF

1 Who was Martin Luther and what did he do at the cathedral door?
2 When was this?
3 What movement did this man begin?
4 What was Loyola's reaction to the Reformers?

The Inquisition

Many terrible things happened between different groups of Christians at this time. Protestants were tortured and killed by Catholics for having a different faith; Protestants tortured and killed Catholics when they got the chance. The Roman Catholic Church had set up in the thirteenth century the **Inquisition**, a special court to judge heresy – not only heretical actions but also intentions. Officials would arrive in an area and preach against heresy. They would offer a period of grace, when heretics could come forward and freely repent. After this, a trial would begin of suspects, and they would be punished.

Two witnesses were required to press charges, and the interviews were held in private. No defence lawyers were allowed, and most people confessed straight away to avoid being tortured and having to spend a long time in prison while their trial was carried out. (Children and old people were given fairly light tortures, and only pregnant women were exempted.) For heresy that was not serious, or committed out of ignorance, there was a light punishment, such as a penance of saying so many prayers or fasting for a period. Serious heretics would have to wear special clothes marking them out and have to pay large fines. They might even lose all their lands. Unrepentant heretics were burned at the stake.

The Inquisition was especially powerful in Spain from the late fifteenth century, where there were large numbers of non-Christians, such as Jews and Muslims, who were suspected of turning people away from the Church by their teachings.

The Protestant splits

The Protestant movement itself split into various factions. The Baptists wanted the right to baptise adults by full immersion in water, irrespective of whether they had been baptised as infants or not. The Presbyterians and Independents wanted no bishops and preferred locally elected ministers.

John Wesley's Methodists wanted to preach in the open air, and they had lay preachers who were not properly ordained ministers. The Church of England would not allow this to carry on, and so Wesley's movement had to become a separate Church, much against his wishes.

Much later the Pentecostals wanted freedom to worship in their own way, using the gifts of the Spirit that they believed God had given them.

New churches are the latest split, when people become unhappy with traditional church life and want to start something new.

▲ John Wesley preaching.

The Anglican Church regards itself as Catholic and Reformed. It opened itself up to some of the ideas of the Reformers, but it continued many Catholic practices. (Henry VIII removed the Pope's authority from England so he could divorce his first wife.) The Church of England is a mixture of Catholic and Protestant, though some people in it are more Catholic or Protestant than others. The Anglican Church is a 'bridge Church', a 'middle way'.

The Church of England is a part of the world-wide Anglican Church, which includes, for example, the Church in Wales and the Church of South Africa, as well as many other national Churches. All Anglican Churches have the Archbishop of Canterbury as their figurehead. A number of bishops run the Church below him, with the help of the priests (also called vicars or rectors) and the people in each parish. A parish is an area under the care of a priest.

Christianity has been in England since Roman times, but the Church of England was separated from the Pope in 1534 when King Henry VIII ruled that the Pope had no authority in the English Church. The British monarch is still governor of the Church, but most decisions are taken by the Church leaders themselves. The monarch is now seen as a guardian or protector of the Church of England. He or she is the most senior layperson, and the Archbishop of Canterbury is the most senior clergyman.

TEST YOURSELF

1 What was the Inquisition?
2 Who were Baptists and who were Pentecostals?
3 Why did the Church of England separate from Rome?

THE GROWTH OF ECUMENISM

KEY QUESTION

What are Christians doing to heal their divisions?

The twentieth century has seen the Churches moving closer together after their bitter disputes in the past. They are remembering that they are all followers of the man from Nazareth, and that they worship the same God. The only way to overcome the arguments of the past is to meet together, to talk and to pray. This does not mean that everyone has to agree with everyone else in every way: people can find where they agree and then respect each other's differences.

▲ **The symbol of the World Council of Churches. The cross is in a boat with the word in Greek for 'one world'. All Christians are in the same world, in 'the same boat', sharing more in common than divides them.**

The World Council of Churches

Dialogue began between the Anglican Church and the Roman Catholic Church in Belgium before the First World War. The horrific experience of this war made many wish to work for unity. In 1925, 37 countries sent Church representatives to a meeting in Stockholm; but it was the aftermath of the Second World War that made more people feel the need to come together. The World Council of Churches (WCC) was set up in 1948, with its headquarters in Geneva. It has over 340 member Churches from over 100 different countries. Its theme is 'All one in Christ'. It had eight international assemblies by 1998. These have been in Amsterdam, Holland, in 1948; Evanston, USA, in 1954; New Delhi, India, in 1961; Uppsala, Sweden, in 1968; Nairobi, Kenya, in 1975; Vancouver, Canada, in 1983; Canberra, Australia, in 1991; and Harare, Zimbabwe, in 1998.

The movement to draw all the Churches closer is called the **ecumenical** movement. The word ecumenical comes from the Greek *oikoumene*, which means one world, or sharing one world.

Vatican II

The Roman Catholic Church was shaken up in the 1960s. Pope John XXIII was elected as a 'caretaker' Pope, for he was already an old man. People did not expect him to do anything new. But he did! In 1962 he opened the Second Vatican Council where many new ideas could be discussed. (The First Vatican Council was in 1869–70.) John XXIII wanted a breath of fresh air to enter the Church, and he hoped for a 'new Pentecost', a new freshness of Christian living in the Church. He died before the Council closed in 1965, but the effects have been far reaching:

- A willingness to work with other Christian groups.
- Changing the services from Latin to the language of the country concerned.
- Commitment to social action in the world.
- Openness to members of other faiths.

One of the fruits of this change was the visit of Pope John Paul II to Britain in 1982. This would have been unthinkable just a generation before.

The Lima document

The World Council of Churches organised a committee of 100 theologians in 1982, representing most of the denominations. They worked on a document, compiled at Lima, in Peru, on the subjects of baptism, Eucharist and ministry. A wide measure of agreement was reached in all three areas, and this document has been called an ecumenical milestone. The basic conclusions were:

- There should be a mutual recognition of each other's baptism as baptism into the one body of Christ, no matter which Church carried it out.
- All Churches should celebrate the Eucharist at least on every Sunday, and members of different Churches should be able to hold joint celebrations of it.
- All Christians should have a share in ministry – it should not all be left to the ordained person. Women should have more roles in

Christian ministry. There is a need for officials like bishops to oversee the Church, and to link it with the faith of the apostles, even in the Free Churches.

It might be some time before all or most of these suggestions are carried out, but modern Christians are far more open to one another than they have possibly ever been in the past.

The Porvoo Declaration

Anglicans and the Baltic Lutherans entered into a new relationship in the 1990s. The Porvoo Declaration decreed that these Lutheran Churches should be equal to the Anglicans, and priests and pastors should recognise each other's ministries as valid and equal. This followed years of dialogue and joint study. Other Lutheran Churches are carrying on dialogue and working closely with Anglicans.

TEST YOURSELF

1 What is the WCC?
2 How many international assemblies did the WCC hold by 1991?
3 What was Vatican II?
4 What is the Lima document?
5 What is the Porvoo Declaration?

RENEWAL IN THE SPIRIT

KEY QUESTION

Why do some Christians speak of a personal experience of the Holy Spirit?

The twentieth century saw the rise of the **charismatic** movement. This wants to see the free and joyful worship of Pentecostal Christians in the mainline Churches. Charismatics stress the work of the Holy Spirit, and say that sharing the Spirit, with a common faith in Jesus, is the real basis of unity. Other differences would then fall into the background.

TASK BOX

The Pope met Robert Runcie, the Archbishop of Canterbury, when he visited England in the 1980s. What changes in the Roman Catholic Church allowed this to happen?

The charismatic movement has influenced the Anglican and Roman Catholic Churches, and most of the Free Churches. The New Church movement is also charismatic in emphasis.

▲ **Charismatic worshippers. Is there any difference in the attitude of the people compared with the photographs of other services?**

Charismatics believe in a personal renewal experience where people become conscious of the Holy Spirit within them. This feels like a deep joy welling up from within, recalling the words of Jesus about the Spirit in John's Gospel: 'The water that I will give him will become in him a spring which will provide him with life-giving water and give him eternal life' (John 4:14 (Good News Bible)).

It might also be accompanied by one of the gifts of the Spirit that Paul mentions. Members of the charismatic movement believe that God has given them certain extraordinary gifts to use to help other people, and to help them to worship. Paul lists these gifts in 1 Corinthians 12:4–11. These are examples of some of the gifts he mentions:

■ *Healing* – through the power of prayer.
■ *Prophecy* – to speak out words that come from an inner sense of what God feels about a situation. They might be words of encouragement, or of warning.
■ *Knowledge* – a person might suddenly have an insight into a person's problem.
■ *Speaking in tongues* – an ability to speak in a language for the purposes of prayer and praise that the speaker has never learned. Some think that these are actual foreign languages. Paul might have something different in mind, though, such as a special prayer language. For some people, this gift seems to be a special subconscious language that enables people to express deep feelings they cannot easily put into words.

These gifts will be used in services and they will also be used in prayer groups held in people's homes. If someone speaks in tongues out loud, then the people will wait to see if someone can interpret the message. Sometimes, people will sing in joyful harmonies in their special language or 'tongue'. This can sound beautiful and heavenly.

The charismatic movement has introduced simple, modern songs into services, as well as the use of instruments like guitars and flutes. It has also stressed the need to feel God's presence within, and for more joy in church life so it is not all serious and sombre. It has also helped to bring many different Christians together – Catholic and Protestant, Anglican and Methodist – in joint prayer groups in people's houses or in large worship meetings in hired halls or churches.

A typical act of charismatic worship would involve:

■ opening, modern praise songs (as well as some traditional hymns) sung one after the other
■ open prayer, with people giving praises and interceding for others
■ gifts of the Spirit, such as prophecy and speaking in tongues
■ testimony about what God has done in someone's life
■ sermon
■ more praise songs
■ during these, there might be the laying on of hands for healing prayer.

A New Approach – Christianity

Some Christians are wary of the movement, though, for at least two reasons:

- There can be a great deal of emotionalism in charismatic worship, which might carry people away with themselves. Crowd emotion can be dangerous.
- Great pressure might be put upon some people to sing out loud, to jump up and down or raise their arms in the air, when that is not their personality. They are quiet and reserved and like to worship in a quieter way.

Not all Christians are happy about the charismatic movement. Yet, despite its extremes and the faults of some of its members, it made a lasting contribution to church life in the twentieth century. Charismatic and Pentecostal Churches are the fastest growing Christian movements.

▲ A group of charismatic worshippers engaged in a healing prayer.

Read this story of healing prayer. The Reverend Colin Urquhart was an Anglican priest who held services of healing. People came to him to be prayed for, and some of them claimed to be healed. A Scottish woman who was losing her hearing because of a childhood illness came for prayer, deeply distressed. Colin Urquhart placed his hands on her and prayed.

We asked the Lord to forgive her, to heal the misery in her life and fill her with the Holy Spirit. She was immediately liberated and began praising and thanking him. It was almost as an afterthought that I placed my hands over her ears: 'Lord, please restore the hearing of your child.' Until then, I had needed to shout to make her hear me when speaking to her...
'Can you hear, now?' I asked quietly.
She turned and looked at me, her face radiant. 'Did you shout then?' she asked.
I went on talking quietly, until my voice was drowned by her saying: 'I can hear, I can hear. Oh, thank you Lord, thank you.'
Colin Urquhart

a Why do some Christians believe the gift of healing is possible?
b How do you react to this? Do you think faith can heal?

Alpha

The Alpha course started at the Anglican parish of Holy Trinity, Brompton, in London in the 1980s. It was developed by the curate, Nicky Gumbel, a former barrister, in the 1990s. This is a teaching course about basic Christianity designed to appeal to all denominations. Alpha, an introductory course to Christian belief, runs for over ten weeks, attendees often meeting for a meal, in a relaxed atmosphere. There is an 'away day' or weekend, where people experience the laying on of hands and prayer for the coming of the Holy Spirit. The course became immensely popular in the late 1990s, with many denominations running it, including the Roman Catholic Church. The books and video material used for its teaching are slick, easy to follow and intelligent. Newcomers are encouraged to ask questions and to discuss doubts, forming friendships in their Alpha groups. The Alpha course has been translated into many languages.

An opportunity to explore the meaning of life.

THE ALPHA COURSE

▲ The Alpha course is an introductory course in Christian belief – designed for people of every denomination.

TASK BOX

a Give as many reasons as you can to explain why the Reformation happened.
b Explain how the WCC has tried to help to unify Churches.
c Explain how Vatican II has helped Catholics to strive for greater unity with other Christians.

TEST YOURSELF

1 What is the charismatic movement?
2 How has this affected attempts to bring different Christians together?
3 List some of the gifts of the Spirit.
4 What is speaking in tongues?

A New Approach – Christianity

1 Describe what is meant by the word apostolic. [2]

2 Explain why bishops are often held in special regard in churches. [8]

3 'All believers should agree with each other.'
Do you agree? Give reasons for your answer and show that you have considered other views. [4]

4 Give an outline of a typical charismatic act of worship. [8]

5 Explain how the charismatic movement helped Christians to worship and meet together. [7]

6 'Changes in Vatican II that allowed Roman Catholics to be involved in activities with other Churches should not have happened.'
Do you agree? Give reasons for your answer, showing that you have considered other points of view. [5]

REMEMBER

▶ Different Churches are not different religions, but denominations.
▶ The Churches split in the eleventh century, and then in the sixteenth century.
▶ The ecumenical movement is trying to reunite the Churches.
▶ The charismatic renewal is a great blessing to many believers and this brings different Christians together in a common experience.

WEBLINKS

The website for the World Council of Churches can be found at
🕷 www.wcc-coe.org

The Alpha website is at
🕷 www.htb.org.uk/alphacourse

7

KEY WORDS

Blessed Sacrament – some of the blessed communion bread reserved after the service is over.
Cantor – a person who leads the singing in an Orthodox church.
Contemplation – silent prayer and reflection; a form of meditation.
Ekklesia – the Assembly, or Gathering – the Greek word for church.
Genuflection – going down on one knee to show respect for the blessed sacrament.
Ichthus – Greek for 'fish' and an early Christian code word, standing for 'Jesus Christ, Son of God, Saviour'.
Incense – scented tree gum burnt in worship.
Jesus Prayer – Orthodox prayer, 'Lord Jesus Christ, Son of God, have mercy on us.'
Peace – a handshake, kiss or an embrace to show that believers all belong to one spiritual family.
Prayer rope – Orthodox Christian rope with many knots. The Jesus Prayer is said on these.
Rosary – a Roman Catholic set of prayer beads with which the Hail Mary prayer is recited.
Sermon – the preaching or address by the minister in a church service.
Sistrum – an Ethiopian Christian rattle.
Stoup – small container for holy water by a church door.
Supplication – a prayer asking for help from God.

KEY QUESTION

What does it mean to worship something?

Worship means to thank God for the gift of life, to spend time on something we feel is worthwhile, to appreciate something that means a great deal to us.

People can worship a hobby, a football team or a pop group. It isn't only religious people who worship! We appreciate and spend time with people and things that are really important to us. Perhaps spiritual worship is deeper and more serious, though. God is holy, and believers can have great devotion and a sense of obedience. Christians worship God in church, or on their own, to give thanks for the gift of life, for what Jesus did, and to feel spiritually refreshed inside.

Christians use a number of things to help them to worship. In a service we will find a combination of some or all of these: actions, words, music and singing, silence, clothes and symbolic objects. Worship is done by the people, and the people are the Church, the *ekklesia* or the Assembly. A common saying goes, 'The Church is the people and not the steeple.' Church buildings can be useful and beautiful places of worship, too, though, and are greatly treasured and respected by the believers.

ACTIONS

The way we move our bodies can express feelings we have. A person who is happy might jump up and down and clap her hands, or a nervous person might twitch his fingers. In a church service, people might kneel down or bow their heads when they say prayers. This is to show respect for God – they are showing that God is greater than them and it helps them to stop feeling proud.

Some people might bow to the cross on the altar at the front of the church, or kneel down on one knee (**genuflection**) before the **Blessed Sacrament** – communion bread that has been kept by the altar after a communion service. Some Christians make the sign of the cross over their bodies to remember that Jesus died for them. Other Christians might prefer to raise their hands when praying or singing. This suggests joy, surrender to God and openness to him. (Opening your arms suggests you are welcoming someone.)

Actions can also involve touch. In many services, people shake hands at one point and say, 'Peace be with you!' This is to express friendship, and to show that all Christians should think of one another as brothers and sisters – even if they do not always live up to that! This action is called the **Peace**.

Loving, caring actions outside a worship service can also be worship to God.

> The King will reply, 'I tell you the truth, whatever you did for one of the least of these brothers of mine, you did for me.'
>
> *Matthew 25:40*

WORDS

Most services will be full of words, spoken or sung. Prayers will be said, and these will either be made up by the people on the spot or read from a Service Book where everyone will join in. Sections from the Bible will always be read out before the whole congregation: often one passage from the Old Testament, one from the letters in the New Testament and one from the Gospels. The Bible is important to Christians as a source of ideas and teachings. They believe they hear God speaking through it in some way: it contains God's Word.

The minister will preach a **sermon**. He, or she, will base this on the Bible passages that were read out. Christians also hope to hear God's word to them through the sermon as the Bible is explained.

KEY QUESTION
What style of music do Christians use in worship?

MUSIC AND SINGING

Music can express deep feelings, and can raise our spirits if we are feeling sad or worried in some way. Also, songs can be a way of showing and of sharing happiness. Music and songs help Christians to praise God. The instruments used may vary from church to church. Some churches have an organ or a piano. Sometimes guitars, flutes or keyboards are used if the songs are more modern and lively.

Traditional hymns sung in churches contain deep meanings and are sung happily by people who understand them or who have been brought up with them. However, the words of some hymns might be difficult, and the tunes seem slow. For this reason, shorter songs have been written, which are being introduced into

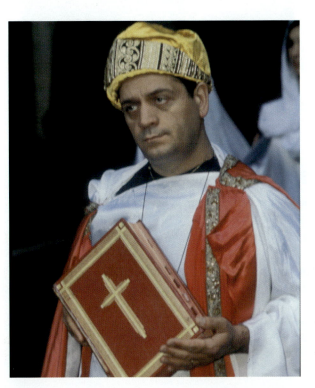

◀ The Gospel reading is the most important reading in many churches. This is based upon the words and actions of Jesus himself. Here, one of the Gospels is carried in procession to show that it is special.

many churches. The words are often based on passages from the Bible, such as this song:

> He is Lord, he is Lord;
> He is risen from the dead, and he is Lord.
> Every knee shall bow, every tongue confess,
> That Jesus Christ is Lord.

(This is based on some words of St Paul in his letter to the Philippians 2:10–11.)

Some churches have no instruments at all – Orthodox Christians sing their services without musical instruments and they have specially trained **cantors** to help with this. Ethiopian Orthodox priests use a gold-coloured instrument called a **sistrum**, which has metal washers threaded on to a metal frame. This is held in the hand and shaken, as the priests sing and move from side to side.

SILENCE

It is wrong to think that Christians have to do things all through a service. Sitting quietly in silence can also be a very important part of worship. It helps all the words and teachings to sink into their minds. It is also a form of meditation, of calming the mind and feeling at peace. Many Christians say that they feel the presence of God with them in these times. This sitting quietly, thinking, praying, or just being still, is called **contemplation**.

a What is being used to make music here, and which type of Christian is this man?

b Which Christian churches have no musical instruments? What do they use instead?

c What modern instruments might be found in many churches today?

d Why are shorter, simpler songs being used rather than traditional hymns in a number of churches today?

How to be still

Find a quiet place. Sit comfortably, so you won't feel like moving for a while. Start to breathe deeper and count your breaths to yourself, up to 20. Listen, for a few moments, to all the sounds around you. Focus on one for a while, and then another. Start to say a word or phrase to yourself, over and over again, such as 'peace', or a saying from the Bible, such as, 'Be still and know that I am God.' Imagine a calm place. Finish by counting 20 more breaths. Then open your eyes and just relax for a while.

▲ A thurible in which incense is burned.

SYMBOLIC OBJECTS

> ### KEY QUESTION
> What symbols are used in churches and in worship?

Many pictures and objects found in churches help people to worship. They are often symbolic. A symbol represents something else, such as a feeling or a truth that is difficult to put into words.

- *Holy water* **Stoup**. Water suggests life and purity. Roman Catholic and some Anglican churches have small containers of holy water by the entrance that people will dip their fingers into and then make the sign of the cross with. Holy water is water that has been blessed by a priest.

- *Incense*. Roman Catholic, Orthodox and some Anglican churches use incense. This is a sweet-smelling spice that is burned with charcoal in a thurible (censer) and wafted around during a service by a person called a thurifer. It produces a pleasant, rich atmosphere and suggests prayers going up to God.

- *Candles and Flowers*. Some churches light candles on the altar. The flickering lights add to the beauty of the church, and light also suggests life and truth, and the presence of God. Flower arrangements in various parts of the church add to the beauty and atmosphere. The colours can remind people of the glory of God and flowers suggest life.

- *Prayer Beads*. Roman Catholic, Orthodox and some Anglican Christians use sets of prayer beads. The Roman Catholic versions are called **rosaries**. The beads are arranged into five groups of ten, with extra beads marking the divisions between these. A short prayer or phrase is said as each bead is slipped through the fingers. This type of prayer can be said in times of silence, when the words can be concentrated on more easily. This prayer is usually said:

Hail Mary, full of grace,
The Lord is with you.
Blessed are you among women,
And blessed is the fruit of your womb, Jesus.
Holy Mary, Mother of God,
Pray for us sinners,
Now and at the hour of our death.

Orthodox **prayer ropes** can have any number of knots in them and the **Jesus Prayer** is recited over and over, establishing a gentle rhythm. The Jesus Prayer is usually 'Lord Jesus Christ, Son of God, have mercy upon us.' This can be shortened in various ways, and might only use the name 'Jesus'.

TASK BOX

a Draw either a Catholic rosary or an orthodox prayer rope.

b Write out the Hail Mary and the Jesus Prayer.

c Why do you think that some find repeating short prayers helpful?

d Is there a saying or word you might use over and over to feel at peace or safe?

e Some Christians criticise this method of prayer by appealing to Matthew 6:7–8. Why is this, and how might someone respond?

PERSPECTIVES

To recite the Rosary is, of course, nothing other than to contemplate, with Mary, the face of Christ.
Cardinal Cormac Murphy O'Connor

And when you pray, do not keep on babbling like pagans, for they think they will be heard because of their many words.
Jesus, Matthew 6:7

For some people, the above two statements are contradictory. To recite the Catholic Rosary is like babbling prayers, saying the Hail Mary over and over again rather like a robot. The Cardinal means something very different. Firstly, a series of stories from the life of Jesus are studied and meditated upon before the Hail Mary is said. There are five Joyful Mysteries (the birth stories), five Sorrowful ones (the Passion), five ones of Light (such as the baptism of Jesus) and five Glorious mysteries (the Resurrection and the coming of the Holy Spirit). The Rosary is like a prayerful Bible study, up to a point.

The saying of the Hail Mary prayer is a rhythm, a gentle way of meditating upon the meaning of the words. It would be wrong to think that God hears you if you say more. The recitation is meant to help calm our souls, not to make God listen.

A New Approach – Christianity

CROSSES AND FISH

An empty cross not only reminds people of the death of Jesus, but also of his resurrection. A crucifix has a carving of the dead Jesus upon it. This helps people to remember his suffering. Some Christians say they find praying in front of a crucifix to be very moving. The initials INRI are often seen above Jesus' head. These stand for 'Jesus of Nazareth, King of the Jews' (in Latin *Iesus Nazarenus Rex Iudaeorum*).

Sometimes there will be various designs hanging on the walls, or on the pulpit or altar. They often stand for something to do with Jesus:

■ IHS – These are the first three letters of the Greek word for Jesus: IHSOYS.

■ The letters above are the first two letters of the Greek word for Christ (ΧΡΙΣΤΟΣ). It is called the chi-rho.
■ The word ΙΧϑΥΣ (pronounced **ichthus**) is Greek for fish. Each letter of this word is the first letter of the words 'Jesus Christ, Son of God, Saviour' in Greek. A simple drawing of a fish was used as a secret sign by the early Christians to avoid being arrested by the Romans. The fish symbolised three things about Jesus and the faith:

1 He was the Saviour of people, the fisher of souls.
2 It suggested the washing of baptism and the new life this brought.
3 The fish suggested sharing. Jesus had shared out fish at the feeding of the five thousand, and had cooked fish for the disciples in John 21. It came to signify the Holy Communion, the meal of bread and wine that was shared in services.

■ The dove is a symbol of God's Spirit. It suggests the peace and tranquillity Christians say they feel in the presence of God.

PRAYER UMBRELLAS AND CROSSES

Ethiopian Orthodox Christians hold highly decorative umbrellas over their priests during special festivals. Besides giving shade from the sun in a hot country, these give a sense of colour

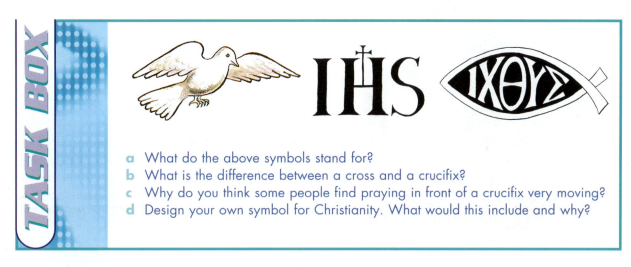

TASK BOX

a What do the above symbols stand for?
b What is the difference between a cross and a crucifix?
c Why do you think some people find praying in front of a crucifix very moving?
d Design your own symbol for Christianity. What would this include and why?

and celebration. There is a suggestion of the protection and shelter of God bringing peace. Crosses, of varying and ornate design, are carried in the processions, too. Worship for the Ethiopian Orthodox is to be visually beautiful.

TEST YOURSELF

1 What is a holy water stoup? Why are these used?
2 Why are candles used in worship?
3 What is incense and why do some use this?
4 Why have flowers in church?
5 Why do Ethiopian Christians use prayer umbrellas?

WHY PRAY?

> ### KEY QUESTION
>
> What do people think prayer actually achieves?

There are four types of prayer: adoration, confession, thanksgiving and supplication.

Adoration

This is when people simply adore God and think about his greatness. God is thought to be vast and endless and the creator of all life. For all their brains and abilities, people are really quite insignificant and there is much more to life and the universe than them. So, a prayer of adoration would be something like, 'O God, how great and marvellous you are!' Or a person might spend time adoring God in silence.

Confession

When people feel that they have done something wrong, or have hurt someone in some way, it is healthy to admit this and face up to it. Confessing to God can help Christians face up to their wrongs. It can also help them to put things right again. Christians believe that God is forgiving and can be turned to for help. The person has to be sincere, though; a prayer of confession is not like just saying sorry and not meaning it.

Thanksgiving

When Christians want to thank God for something, this is a prayer of thanksgiving. It might be for some good news they have heard, or for getting better after an illness, or simply for the gift of life itself. It can help people to feel grateful, and it helps to stop them taking things for granted.

Supplication

Supplication means asking for help. People might pray for one of their own needs, such as for the strength to do a difficult job, or to have the courage to stand up and be counted over some issue. Or it could be that they pray for the needs of others, for a family that has little money or for a sick friend. It could be a prayer for the whole world, such as one against famine or war.

DOES PRAYER WORK?

People can either feel a sense of guidance or a presence when they pray, a deep peace within, or they feel that a problem is solved.

A sense of a presence or deep joy

This can happen quite suddenly, during a time of personal prayer at home, or in a church service. It can even happen when the person is not doing anything religious.

One person wrote: 'I began praying, not really sure that there was a God. ... A great relaxation came upon my mind and everything fitted together. It only lasted for a moment, perhaps four to five seconds ... I really felt that God was communicating with me.'

Another person recalled: 'In adolescence, after receiving instruction for confirmation, one day in church I prayed for Christ to come into my life. A sense of relief, the peace of God, something fantastic.'

John Hick, a professor of theology, has written about an incident that happened when he was a student:

It happened ... of all places – on the top deck of a bus in the middle of the city of Hull, when I was a Law student at University College, Hull. ... It was as though the skies opened up and light poured down and filled me with a sense of overflowing joy in response to an immense transcendent goodness and love. I remember that I couldn't help smiling broadly – smiling back, as it were, at God – though if any of the other passengers were looking they must have thought that I was a lunatic, grinning at nothing. And there have been a number of less intense, usually much less intense, moments from time to time, varying from a background sense to a momentarily more specific sense of existing in the unseen presence of God.

Guidance from God

Some Christians feel that God guides them in making a major decision by popping sudden ideas or thoughts into their minds. This might feel like an inner voice, or an inner prompting. It might just be a sudden idea that appears as if from nowhere and makes everything click together. One example involved Dr Frances Young, a teacher at Birmingham University, who was ordained a Methodist minister on 3 July 1984. This is how she describes her decision to be ordained:

I was driving home and stopped at the traffic lights in Dudley, and suddenly I had another loud thought which was simply, 'You should get ordained.' An extraordinary thing happened after that. I just don't know how I drove back – I'm not aware of the journey at all – I must have been on automatic pilot or something. ... But during the course of that drive home ... I had the whole of my life laid out in front of me; and all its peculiar twists and turns which hadn't seemed to make very much sense suddenly fell into a pattern, as though this was all leading up to that moment and that conclusion.

Inner promptings or flashes of insight seem to help some Christians work out the direction of their lives.

Cured by faith

The Gospels are full of stories of healing miracles. People have claimed to be healed in this way in recent times as well. You have heard about the Rev. Colin Urquhart in Unit Six. Here is another case, which is related in his book *When the Spirit Comes*:

> A man seriously ill with cancer came to a prayer group in the vicarage lounge, and the people prayed for him. Nothing seemed to have happened. He had not felt any change. But when he went into hospital a few days later, it was discovered that all the cancer tumours had disappeared.

There are other stories of healings that are gradual or incomplete, rather than split second 'cure-all' miracles. For example, the Roman Catholic James Moon went to Lourdes with his wife. Lourdes is a shrine where many pilgrims go to pray for healing (see p149). He was suffering from a stroke and diabetes. He could hardly walk, and was put in the baths there. He suddenly felt a strange feeling come over him, and he knew that he could walk. He did so, much to everyone's amazement, but still dragged a foot and was told to be careful. He had not been completely healed.

Christians have different ways of understanding such healings. Some think that God intervenes in the normal course of nature to do something amazing and new. It is a force that cannot be investigated by science.

Other Christians think that the power of faith, of belief, itself sometimes unlocks certain powers in a person's mind and body that science is only just coming to realise exist. The presence of God helps to create the faith necessary to unlock these abilities. James Moon, for example, suddenly felt that he believed he could walk. Jesus often told people, 'Your faith has cured you.'

Marvellous though these stories are, some people pray for healing and nothing seems to happen. They stay sick, suffer and sometimes die. Prayer might help them feel stronger emotionally, so that they can cope with their illness better. It does not affect their physical condition at all, though. It gives an inner peace and strength, and most people who ask for healing prayer probably experience something like this.

None of the experiences mentioned in this chapter are claimed as out-and-out proofs of the existence of God. A sceptic could argue that the loud thoughts and joyful presences are all created by the person's own mind. Also, people might get well because they strongly want to.

Christians would respond that it feels different from things happening in their own minds, that it is not like forgotten thoughts popping into their memories again. The sense of a presence, they say, feels like something or someone else being with them.

Also, the result of all these experiences is often a deep change in the person concerned. They are not just weird experiences – they claim that they alter a person's outlook, and usually change him or her for the better. So, a person feeling an inner prompting might do something very brave that he or she would never have dreamed of doing alone, or a person healed through prayer will feel spiritually refreshed within, as well as physically better. It is all a matter of faith: of what a person believes. There is no direct proof of God in these experiences, but Christians argue that there is no proof that God is not involved either.

Summing up

The idea that prayer gives a person a sense of perspective is a very important one for Christians. Christians feel that prayer helps them to live their lives by providing an opportunity to step aside from the hustle and bustle of everyday life, by seeking quietness, peace of mind and guidance. It helps them to feel refreshed within. One Christian poet summed this up when he wrote, 'There lives the dearest freshness deep down things.'

WEBLINKS

A site exploring Christian symbols can be found at
http://home.att.net/ ~wegast/symbols/symbols.htm

An interactive site about prayer is at
www.rejesus.co.uk/spirituality/ post_prayer

TASK BOX

a Bring a couple of old umbrellas into the class. Decorate these with Christian symbols. Write out some examples of Christian prayers and attach these with cotton from the edges of the umbrella. Display these along with photos of Ethiopian Christian prayer umbrellas.

b Using a roll of plain wallpaper, draw a Christian symbol using marker pens. Then write a few words of explanation underneath.

REMEMBER

- Worship can involve actions, words, silence, music and symbols.
- Some prefer to use informal, modern styles of worship and some use traditional forms.
- Symbols suggest the presence and beauty of God – such as candlelight, fresh flowers and incense.
- Prayer has different aspects and some feel that prayers are really answered by an inner feeling, a sense of peace, inner guidance or changed circumstances.

---

1 Describe two Christian symbols that might be used in worship. [2]
2 Explain what these stand for and how are they used. [6]
3 Explain the difference between thanksgiving and supplication when praying. [4]
4 'Prayer changes things.'
   Do you agree? Give reasons for your opinion, showing you have considered other points of view. [8]
5 Describe four different types of prayer. [8]
6 Explain how prayer can also involve stillness and quiet. [7]
7 'Prayer cannot change things.'
   Do you agree? Give reasons for your point of view and show consideration of those of others. Refer to Christian beliefs and experiences in your answer. [5]

Assignment

UNIT EIGHT | Gathering together: buildings and their function

8

KEY WORDS

Altar – the holy table upon which the bread and wine are blessed.

Baptism – pouring water over someone, or immersing someone in water in the name of the Trinity.

Baptistry – a small pool in a Baptist church.

Cathedral – a large church where the bishop is based.

Chancel – the area of some churches where the choir sits.

Consubstantiation – Luther's belief that the substance of bread and wine remained, joined to the substance of the body and blood of Christ.

Encolpion – medallion worn by an Orthodox bishop with a picture of Mary on it.

Eucharist – Greek for thanksgiving. A thanksgiving meal using bread and wine, or Holy Communion.

Font – the place where people are baptised.

Holy Communion – sharing bread and wine to remember the death and resurrection of Jesus.

Iconostasis – a screen covered with icons in front of an Orthodox altar.

Lectern – the stand where the Bible is kept.

Narthex – the entrance hall of an Orthodox church.

Pulpit – a raised platform from where the sermon is traditionally preached.

Royal Doors – the doors leading to the altar in the iconostasis.

Transignification – a modern idea among some Roman Catholics to explain how bread and wine become the body and blood. They change their significance in the minds of the worshippers.

Transubstantiation – the traditional Roman Catholic view that the substance of bread and wine changes into that of the body and blood of Christ.

KEY QUESTION

Are church buildings in any way special to worshippers?

CHURCH BUILDINGS

Church buildings can be purely functional – a hall to assemble in – or they can be highly symbolic. Remember that the Church is the people, but the place where they worship is treated with great reverence by many.

The traditional style of English parish churches was intended to give the worshipper the sense of being on a journey through life. You stepped through the door where the **font** was placed and people were baptised. You walked along to take a seat or to stand in the main assembly area. There you listened to the service, and then went forward to take the bread and wine at the **altar**, the holy place where only the priest and his helpers would stand. This represented the goal of life – moving forwards and joining God after death. The service was like a symbol, or a rehearsal for life's journey through the outside world.

Modern churches tend to be designed in different ways. The problem with the old style of building was that it was like being on a train journey, with the driver at the front, and you did not see much of the people in front of you, except the backs of their heads. One idea has been to bring the altar, or Lord's Table, further forward, so seats can be arranged to the sides of it. Then the minister stands in amongst the people.

Some new churches are circular, so that the people can see each other more easily. This tries to create a more friendly atmosphere. The Roman Catholic **Cathedral** in Liverpool (the Metropolitan Cathedral of Christ the King) is a good example of this: the seats are in a circle with the altar in the middle and there are side chapels around the perimeter. This new style emphasises that God is close to people and with them in everyday life. People sit round the altar, looking at each other, and feeling that God is at the centre.

▲ The opening service of the Roman Catholic Cathedral in Liverpool in 1967. What things in the design suggest togetherness as well as the greatness of God?

The old style buildings stressed the idea that God is very different from people, and gave the idea that God is very great by making him seem far away, with the altar right at the other end of the church from the people. Great Cathedrals emphasised this even more, with their wide spaces and huge ceilings.

Modern churches do not always lose a sense of God's greatness, though, as in the Liverpool Roman Catholic Cathedral where the tower that sweeps up above the altar gives a sense of height and distance.

NEAR OR FAR?

One of the key ideas of the Christian faith is that God became man in Jesus. The incarnation teaches that God humbled himself to step into his creation. God came close. Yet, many traditional church buildings show the very opposite. Here, God seems distant and ultra holy. Modern styles, with people gathering around a table, try to get back to the central idea of the incarnation.

Perhaps too much Christian worship was

modelled on the royal court – ranks of officials and a great distance between you and the monarch. This style crept in when the Roman emperors adopted Christianity as the faith of the Roman Empire. Before that, churches and worship gatherings were much simpler. Early meeting places were converted houses with the lounge/dining hall being used for worship. People would gather around the table.

Many Free churches are simple in design and have few symbolic objects inside – perhaps only a cross and a hanging showing a dove or the IHS symbol. This is because some Christians feel that too many objects are a distraction. God is invisible and should be felt inside the mind and listened to in the words of the Bible. They might also fear that some more superstitious people might start to worship pictures and statues instead of God (see the second commandment, Exodus 20:4–5.) Interestingly, archaeologists have found that old Jewish synagogues had decorated walls, often with scenes from Bible stories. The Jews would definitely not have worshipped these images, though.

There seem to be two different types of character amongst Christians, therefore: those who like simple worship with few decorations, and those who prefer to worship with an abundance of colourful sights, smells and sounds.

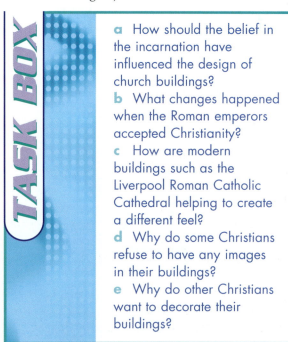

TASK BOX

a How should the belief in the incarnation have influenced the design of church buildings?

b What changes happened when the Roman emperors accepted Christianity?

c How are modern buildings such as the Liverpool Roman Catholic Cathedral helping to create a different feel?

d Why do some Christians refuse to have any images in their buildings?

e Why do other Christians want to decorate their buildings?

EXAMPLES OF CHURCH BUILDINGS

An Anglican parish church

A typical Anglican parish church will have a nave, a **chancel** (or choir) and a sanctuary area:

- The nave is where the people gather and sit.
- The chancel is for the choir.
- The sanctuary is where the priest and altar servers stand and the **Holy Communion** is blessed at the altar.

The **pulpit** is a raised platform where the sermon is often preached from. The **lectern** is a stand that holds the Bible. Traditionally, this is in the form of a brass eagle. The eagle symbolises the word of God flying forth to the people from the Bible. The font is where people are baptised. The altar is where the bread and wine are blessed.

There will be crosses and candlesticks as well as colourful banners or hangings.

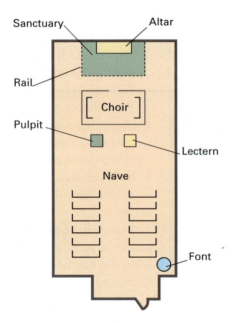

Parish Church

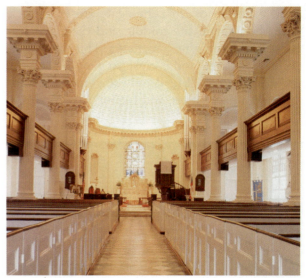

▲ **The interior of an Anglican church.**

A Roman Catholic church

A Roman Catholic church will have a nave and a sanctuary. There will be a pulpit, a lectern, a font and an altar as in the Anglican churches. There might be more decoration – more candles, statues of Jesus, Mary and the saints. There will be a stand where small candles are lit when people say a prayer (votive candles).

There will always be a tabernacle – a small safe containing blessed communion bread. This will have a special candle burning beside it, a sanctuary light.

In older Catholic churches there will usually be confessional boxes – private places where priests can hear people's confessions.

▲ **The interior of a Roman Catholic church.**

▲ The interior of a Methodist church.

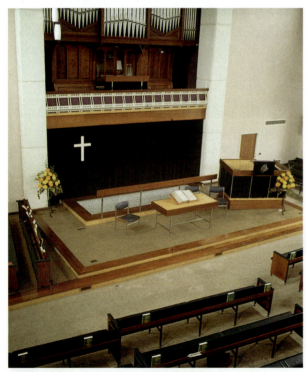

▲ The interior of a Baptist church.

A Methodist church

Methodist churches are simpler, with a gathering area and a raised platform for the pulpit and the holy table. Older-style buildings will have a tall pulpit and a small table in front of it. This emphasises the importance of the Bible and preaching that is central to Methodist worship. Holy communion is celebrated more infrequently.

A Baptist church

Baptist churches are also simple and can be set out like a Methodist church with the pulpit and the smaller table at the front. The whole building is called a sanctuary, and not just the area around the holy table. This emphasises that the whole gathering is sacred, and God is in every section of the building equally.

One special feature is a **baptistry**, a small pool boarded over for normal services. Baptist believers will only baptise older children and adults – in other words, people who can speak for themselves rather than infants.

New churches

New churches are Free churches and charismatic. They probably started out in houses or in rented halls – such as local school halls. A building may then be purchased when they gather enough people and funds have been gathered. These buildings are plain and functional – just meeting halls. There will be a stage area for a worship band and for the leaders.

TEST YOURSELF

1 What are the nave, chancel and sanctuary?
2 What are an altar, a lectern, a pulpit and a font used for?
3 Which churches have a baptistry and why?
4 Why do some churches have a pulpit that is taller than the holy table?

FOCUS ON THE ORTHODOX CHURCH

Orthodox church buildings are very ornate and try to create a sense of the holy and otherworldly by their use of colour and decoration. They are places of great reverence and are divided up into an entrance hall (**narthex**), a gathering space and the sanctuary, or holy place. Traditionally, they are built in a square design with a domed roof.

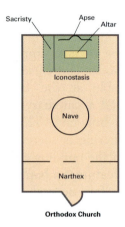

Orthodox Church

The layout

The narthex represents this world: ordinary society. A person steps from this into the nave or gathering area. The nave represents the kingdom of heaven, where people are forgiven, saved and God dwells with them. The ceiling or dome represents heaven. This is the beyond, the eternal, and the circle of the dome suggests eternity, going round and round for ever. The blue and gold of the dome, with pictures of Christ and the angels, represents heaven.

The rectangular building reminds us that all the earth is represented there, the four corners, all nations. All are equal in the worship space. The nave faces east, where the altar, or holy table, is situated. The east is the position of the rising sun and it is an ancient symbol of blessing and the presence of God. In Christianity, it is a symbol of the resurrection.

There are few seats in an average Orthodox church. Some line the walls for the aged and infirm. Most people stand. They have a freedom to move around because of this. They can bow, cross themselves, kneel or lie full length (prostrate) on the ground as they please. They are free to come and go, to move around the church. There are no seated rows to disturb.

Services are long and very traditional, often being composed in the fourth century CE. Despite this, people are also free to worship in their own way. It is not uncommon for one person to be prostrate with others standing around him (or her). Or, someone might walk up to an icon (a holy painting) and spend several minutes before this, saying their prayers, oblivious to anything else happening around them.

The holy icons

Icons (from the Greek word meaning 'image') are sacred paintings that decorate the walls and dome of Orthodox churches. These are of Jesus, Mary, the holy angels or the saints. The characters have haloes of light, and light shining from their faces to suggest the presence of God within

PERSPECTIVES

A church is 'always turned toward the East whence Christ came, like a ship it floats ... and sails towards the East, towards Christ'.
Paul Evdokimov, an Orthodox theologian

The 'east' in ancient religions was a symbol of life and blessing. This was because the sun rose in the east.

The rising sun was a symbol of the resurrection in early Christianity. Why do you think this was?

Why does all the action and worship in Orthodox churches face east?

A New Approach – Christianity

▲ A Greek Orthodox Patriarch kisses an icon of the Virgin Mary in a church in Istanbul.

them. The image of Jesus on the dome is called 'Christ Pantocrator'. This means 'Christ the ruler and creator of all'. Orthodox Christians show great reverence to these holy images, bowing, crossing themselves and praying before them. They will have an icon corner in their homes, too, where they will say their prayers. Icons are like sacraments, physical things that convey a spiritual presence. It is not actually the paintings that are honoured, but what they represent. They are often called 'windows into heaven'.

The iconostasis

The **iconostasis** is a large screen that separates the sanctuary from the nave. This has many rows of icons and three doorways. The central

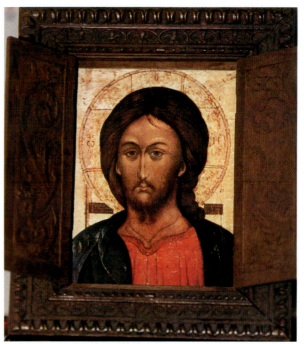

▲ What does the golden halo in this icon suggest about the importance of Christ?

doorway has two doors known as the **Royal Doors**. These lead directly to the holy table. There are scenes of the angel appearing to Mary, and of the four Gospel writers (evangelists) on these. Pictures of Jesus, Mary, John the Baptist, angels, the apostles, Old Testament prophets and various saints will adorn the rest of the screen.

One other doorway leads to the vestry. This is where the priests and servers dress and the book

▲ An iconostasis, showing the Royal Doors.

of the Gospels is kept. This door opens and the Gospel is brought out among the people in the services. The third door leads to the Chapel of Preparation. The bread and the wine are prepared here. Orthodox Christians use real bread for communion.

Two large candelabras hang in front of the iconostasis. These represent the pillar of fire and the cloud that led the Hebrews through the desert in the book of Exodus. The lights remind Orthodox Christians that God guides them today.

The holy table

The holy table, or altar, is cubelike and has various decorative objects upon it. There is a seven-branched candlestick (as in Judaism) representing the sevenfold gifts of God. There is also a container for blessed bread and wine, the tabernacle, and a lit candle suspended above this, 'the Eternal Light'. Sometimes there are two circles standing beside the tabernacle with paintings of six-winged angels upon them. These represent the angels in the book of Revelation who dwell close to the throne of God. Orthodox Christians will bow and cross themselves when they are near the altar to honour the presence of Christ in the holy bread and wine in the tabernacle.

Above the holy table will be an icon of Mary with the Christ child shown within her. She has her hands raised in prayer and worship. This is known as the Orans, 'the Praying person'. This icon reminds the worshipper that the church exists only because of the incarnation of God in Jesus.

▲ An Orans (a person praying) icon of Mary, with Christ shown within her. Why does she have her hands raised?

The throne

The bishop's throne stands behind the altar. This is his seat, reminding people that the bishop is the head of the local church. Each congregation is part of a greater assembly and family. An icon of Christ as the High Priest is painted upon the throne, and the bishop will usually wear a circular headdress modelled on eastern crowns. He also carries a shepherd's crook on top of which is a symbol of Jesus. This is a circle with Greek letters Chi-Rho representing the name 'Christ' and the Alpha and the Omega letters. He would also wear a medallion around his neck, an **encolpion**, with a picture of Mary upon it. For the Orthodox, Mary is a symbol of the Church, of all the people.

The clergy

Orthodox priests wear similar robes at the **Eucharist** to Anglicans and Roman Catholics, though of a slightly different design. They have the alb, chasuble and stole. Otherwise they have black or grey cassocks. Some have special hats, such as the Greek clergy. Other types of ancient Orthodox Church clergy have more elaborate headgear. Armenian clergy are hooded and Syrians have caps covered with crosses.

A New Approach – Christianity

▲ The various robes of Orthodox priests, including the colourful chasuble and stole similar to Anglican and Roman Catholic priests (see page 122 also).

(see page 122 also)

THE CHURCH ASSEMBLED

Baptism

Baptism is a sign of an inner cleansing, a forgiveness that comes from God through Jesus. It is also a sign of turning over a new leaf, of 'dying' to an old way of life and 'rising' to a new one. The word 'baptise' in Greek means to be submerged or plunged underneath. Going under the water suggests dying, and coming up suggests rising.

Orthodox, Roman Catholic, Anglican, Lutheran, United Reformed and Methodist Churches baptise infants. The Orthodox actually put them under the water in a large font three times. The others pour water over their heads three times, for Father, Son and Holy Spirit. People are baptised in the name of the Trinity.

Some Free Churches such as Baptists and Pentecostals will only baptise people who are old enough to speak for themselves.

Baptism is seen by many who accept infant baptism as a way of bringing God to the human

▲ Baptism usually takes place in a font, a container in which water is blessed.

Do you turn to Christ as Saviour?
I turn to Christ.
Do you submit to Christ as Lord?
I submit to Christ.
Do you come to Christ, the way, the truth
and the life?
I come to Christ.

Personal conversion

Other Christians feel that baptism alone is not important in itself; that it is just a sign. A person needs to have a conversion experience. This happens when people come to believe that Jesus died for them personally. They feel challenged to submit their lives to him and to ask God for forgiveness. They say they feel a sense of new life within and they believe that they will eventually

soul, to help cut off the evil influences in the world. Some think this helps by washing away original sin inherited from 'Adam', and others just see this as a loving channel for God's Spirit to work in the soul.

This is only the beginning of the process, though, as people need to go on responding to God throughout their lives, and opening themselves to his Spirit. Baptism starts a good work, but it must be completed by personal acts of faith later.

There are different understandings of baptism among Christians. Some Christians believe that baptism is just a sign, a symbol of a personal decision to follow Jesus. Others believe that it is one of the sacraments, being an action that conveys a blessing in itself.

Remember, too, that some Christians are baptised as infants when they do not know what is happening to them. Others are baptised when they are older and able to make a definite confession of faith for themselves. Infants are baptised on trust, as parents and godparents make promises for them. These are some of the promises from the Church of England rite:

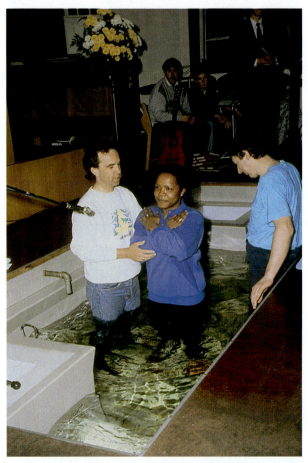

▲ Some churches only baptise people old enough to speak for themselves. They are usually put underneath the water in a pool – this is total submersion.

▲ Orthodox Christians lower candidates under the water in the font three times, each one for the Father, the Son and the Holy Spirit.

go to heaven because Jesus died for their sins. Salvation, in this view, is still a process, though, and not an 'instant mashed potato' idea, for people are not made good and perfect overnight. People need to respond to God for the rest of their lives. Salvation is a process of sanctification (being made holy, or complete) that is lifelong, even if it has a clear and a definite start.

TASK BOX

a There are different ideas about what baptism does. Explain these, covering:
- the sin of Adam
- inner cleansing and the love of God
- a sign of an inner change, of a personal decision

b Should babies be baptised? Give reasons for your answer.

◄ Some people respond to calls to be saved by evangelists such as Billy Graham. This is a moment of decision for them, a turning point in their lives.

Confirmation

Confirmation is a rite some Christians have in order to allow people to make a personal commitment to Jesus if they have been baptised as an infant, when they could not speak for themselves. They repeat the promises made for them at their baptism and a bishop lays his hands on their heads and prays for the Holy Spirit to bless them. Usually, holy oil is used called *chrism*. This is olive oil containing scent, which is blessed by the bishop. It symbolises the Holy Spirit.

Orthodox Christians do not have confirmation as such, even though they have infant baptism. They have *chrismation*. This is where a priest uses oil of chrism and prays for the Spirit's blessing upon the candidate after their baptism.

Free Churches such as the Baptists often have a laying on of hands after a believer's baptism, too, asking for the blessing of the Spirit.

Holy Communion

There is one action that is very important in most Christian worship: Holy Communion. This is where bread and wine are shared out. This is done because of the Last Supper that Jesus had with

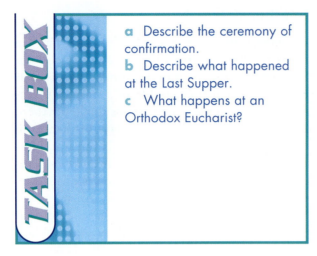

TASK BOX

a Describe the ceremony of confirmation.
b Describe what happened at the Last Supper.
c What happens at an Orthodox Eucharist?

▲ **The bread suggests the body of Jesus, the wine his blood. Christians remember his death but also celebrate his risen presence.**

his disciples. On the night before his arrest he gathered his disciples into an upper room in Jerusalem, and ate a special meal with them. This was probably the Passover meal that the Jews eat once a year. It is a meal that remembers the time when the ancestors of the Jews were slaves in Egypt, nearly 1300 years before the time of Jesus. Jews believe that God sent Moses to set their ancestors free and they remember this event each year with this special meal. It consists of bread and wine and other symbolic items. At the Last Supper Jesus took the bread and wine and shared them with his disciples, giving the bread and wine a new meaning. The earliest account of this is in one of St Paul's letters, 1 Corinthians 11:23–6, and a version of it is also in the first three Gospels: 'While they were eating, Jesus took bread, gave thanks and broke it, and gave it to his disciples, saying, "Take it; this is my body." Then he took the cup, gave thanks and offered it to them, and they all drank from it. "This is my blood of the covenant which is poured out for many," he said to them' (Mark 14:22–4).

Jesus took the bread and the wine in the Passover meal and made it refer to himself: the bread was his body, and the wine was his blood. Christians have shared out bread and wine ever since. The early Church used to share it as part of a full meal that everyone had. This was called the *agape* feast (*agape* is a Greek word for love). This is not always practical now that there are many more people in churches. Some Churches, such as Roman Catholics, Orthodox and Anglicans, share the bread and the wine at least

each week (with some having daily Holy Communions). Independent (Free) churches, however, tend to share it once or twice a month. The Salvation Army and the Society of Friends (also known as the Quakers) are Christian groups who do not share out bread and wine. They stress that faith is an inner affair of the heart and they do not need any sacraments. The Society of Friends stress that Jesus is present at every meal between believers.

Real bread and real wine?

Jesus used bread and wine, and so Holy Communion must use these foodstuffs (and not beer and rice, for example). However, some use unleavened bread. This is often made in small wafers that are easy to count out and to distribute. Others use leavened bread and break off small chunks. Many Roman Catholics and Anglicans use wafers, as they believe that the bread and the wine are holy things only after

PERSPECTIVES

> An Orthodox priest was once asked how he coped with leavened bread when celebrating communion. If he believed that it became, in some sense, the body and blood of Christ, was he not afraid of dropping crumbs? He replied, 'Well we clear up as carefully as we can, and if there are any crumbs, I'm sure God can cope with a few crumbs!'

they are blessed. Orthodox Christians use leavened bread, though. They cut out a square section of the bread that is brought up to the altar. This section (known as the Lamb) is blessed and broken up into the chalice of wine. Communion is given together, on a spoon. The rest of the bread is given out to anyone who wishes to eat it, including non-Orthodox visitors.

Some Free churches use non-alcoholic wine to protect the consciences of anyone who does not drink alcohol or who might have a drink problem. Others stress that Jesus would have used fermented wine, though this would have been well watered down.

TEST YOURSELF

1 What is meant by the Last Supper?
2 What was the Passover?
3 Where is the earliest account of the Last Supper found?
4 Why was the story of the death and resurrection written down so early?

The meaning of Holy Communion

The bread and wine remind Christians of the death of Jesus, but also of his resurrection. Bread can stand for life (it is the basic foodstuff) and wine can stand for joy (it is used for celebrations).

Different Churches call this meal by different names, such as Holy Communion, the Eucharist, the Mass, the Lord's Supper, the Divine Liturgy and the Breaking of Bread. There are also different ways that Christians understand the meal:

- Some see it as just a *symbol*, where the bread and wine stand for the body and blood. It is a reminder, a visual aid.
- Others think that *Jesus is spiritually present* in the bread and wine, and that, in some sense, it becomes his body and blood.

Whether Christians see the Holy Communion as bringing Jesus' presence to them, or simply as a visual aid to remember the death and resurrection of Jesus, they all agree that it is a Eucharist, a 'thanksgiving' meal, to translate the Greek. It is a way of sharing with one another. Eating is a basic human activity, and sharing food can break down barriers between people and strengthen friendships. Besides this, they can celebrate the centre of their faith – the love of God shown in the story of the death and resurrection of Jesus. It is thought that the earliest parts of the Gospels to be written down were the story of the Passion – the death and resurrection of Jesus. These would have been used at Eucharists all over the ancient world.

Whatever Christians believe exactly about the Holy Communion, they share the same beliefs about Jesus in common and what it represents at heart. God became man and he died and rose again to save humanity. Many different churches allow members of other churches to share in their communion, but some have strict rules. The Roman Catholic and the Orthodox Churches usually allow only their own members to receive. They feel that to be in communion with them is to share the same faith without division.

The following photographs show how different Churches celebrate Holy Communion, and suggest their different beliefs about it. What do you think these different Churches believe about the eucharist they are celebrating? Note how some have many small cups of wine and all wait to drink together, and some have a common cup that they all have a sip from.

a   Roman Catholic Mass
b   Informal – Greenbelt or housegroup of New Church communion
c   Pentecostal Communion

A New Approach – Christianity

WEBLINKS

Websites for the Roman Catholic Church, the Anglican Church, the Orthodox Churches, the Methodist Church, the United Reformed Church and the Baptist Church can be found as follows:

 www.catholic-ew.org.uk

🕷 www.CofE.org.uk

🕷 www.bbc.co.uk/religion/
religions/christianity/
subdivisions/orthodox/
index.shtml

🕷 www.methodost.org.uk

🕷 www.urc.org.uk

🕷 www.baptist.org.uk

REMEMBER

- Some church buildings are very plain and some are very ornate.
- Some Christians believe in having images of Christ and the saints in churches.
- Orthodox Christians have a special reverence for holy icons.
- Holy Communion is practised by all the Christian Churches.
- There are very different understandings of Holy Communion.

1 What other name can be used for the Eucharist? [2]
2 Describe the main features of one particular Christian place of worship. [6]
3 Explain why Christians are baptised. [8]
4 'Jesus is present in Holy Communion.'
   Do you agree? Give reasons for your opinion and show that you have considered other points of view. In your answer, you should refer to the beliefs of Christians. [4]

Assignment

KEY WORDS

Abortion – the termination of a pregnancy.
Agape – Greek word for 'love' meaning costly, suffering love.
Alb – long, white robe worn by Christian priests.
Annulment – where a marriage is declared never to have properly taken place.
Chasuble – a colourful poncho-style robe worn by priests at the Eucharist.
Committal – when a coffin is lowered into a grave, or the curtain closes at the crematorium. This is a final handing over to God.
Consent – the part of the marriage service where the couple are asked if it is their intention that the vows are to be exchanged.
Deacon – Greek for 'server'.
Episkopos – Greek for 'overseer' or bishop.
Excommunicated – not allowed to receive holy communion.
Presbyter – Greek for 'elder' or priest.
Registrar – a person authorised to perform a marriage and sign the register.
Stefana – the crowns used in an Orthodox marriage service.
Stole – colourful scarf worn by Christian priests.
Surplice – a long, white robe used by some clergy.
Vocation – a personal calling to be a Christian minister or to live in a religious community as a monk or nun.
Vows – special, sacred promises made by the bride and groom.

KEY QUESTION

How does the Church help to build a sense of community in marriage and in funerals?

There are points in people's lives when they feel that they have passed from one stage of life to another. This might seem gradual or sudden. Some societies and religions have special ceremonies to mark these changes. They are called rites of passage. Family and friends can then join in the celebrations when someone passes from one stage to another. It helps it to sink in for all concerned, and helps people to think about the meaning of the various stages of life. Christianity has a series of rites of passage that form a cycle for life. We are concerned, here, mainly with marriage and death.

Life Cycle: Birth → Adulthood → Marriage → Old Age → Death → Birth

MARRIAGE

People can be married in a register office but Christians are expected to marry in church. Most ministers of religion are authorised to perform marriages, but some Independent (or Free) Church ministers are not, and they have to ask a civil **registrar** to attend the service and sign certain documents.

The preparation

A couple wishing to be married will visit the minister and talk things over with him. He might arrange a few meetings, to try to get to know them a little. He will try to make sure that they understand what a serious step marriage is, and will answer any of their questions. They will read through the service, and rehearse this. They will consider the **vows** (or promises) which they are about to make.

The service

There are certain traditions within weddings, such as the bride wearing white, and the father giving her away during the service. These do not have to be followed, though, if the people are not happy with them. There are parts of the service that cannot be changed, such as the couple exchanging their vows, or the minister pronouncing them man and wife. A marriage service has to have certain contents:

- The minister asks if there is any reason, in law, why the people should not marry.
- The couple have to give their **consent** to each other before witnesses.
- The couple exchange the marriage vows before witnesses.
- The couple are proclaimed as husband and wife.
- The register has to be signed, as a legal record of the marriage.

The giving of a ring, or rings, is usual, but not essential. The most sacred part of the ceremony is the exchange of vows. This is what actually marries you.

The consent

The minister says to the bridegroom, 'John, will you take Sally to be your wife? Will you love her, comfort her, honour and protect her, and, for-saking all others, be faithful to her as long as you both shall live?'

Then he says to the bride, 'Sally, will you take John to be your husband? Will you love him, comfort him, honour and protect him, and, for-saking all others, be faithful to him as long as you both shall live?'

Hopefully, they will both answer 'I will' to these questions. They can still call everything off at this point if they are having doubts!

TEST YOURSELF

1. What is the consent?
2. What are the vows?
3. Why have rings?
4. What needs to be signed?

The vows

The bridegroom says, 'I, John, take you, Sally, to be my wife, to have and to hold from this day forward; for better, for worse, for richer, for poorer, in sickness and in health, to love and to cherish, till death us do part, according to God's holy law; and this is my solemn vow.'

The bride either says the same back to the bridegroom, or a slightly different version in which she promises 'to love, cherish and obey'. This is regarded as old-fashioned by many modern couples. In the past the man was thought to be the head of the household, and the wife was subordinate to him. Some still choose this; if they do, the bridegroom will then add that he will worship his wife. The vows are made to each other, before God.

The ring(s)

The ring is then presented, and the bridegroom says to the bride, 'I give you this ring as a sign of our marriage. With my body I honour you, all that I am I give to you, and all that I have I share with you, within the love of God, Father, Son and Holy Spirit.'

The ring is a token of the love between the couple and is worn as a reminder by the bride (and maybe the bridegroom as well). It is also a symbol of eternity, being a circle – a symbol of unending love.

After the giving of the ring, the minister says, 'I therefore proclaim that they are husband and wife.' And then adds, 'That which God has joined together, let no one put asunder.'

The Orthodox Church

Orthodox wedding services are slightly different. The couple exchange rings at an engagement before the wedding. The priest blesses the couple, and there is a party afterwards. During the wedding service itself, a silver crown (a **stefana**), or a garland, is held over each of their heads. These are then placed on their heads, the priest joins their hands and he blesses their future life together. Almond sweets are shared out, and then there is a full feast.

TASK BOX

a What is happening in this picture and why?
b What does a ring symbolise?
c Would a marriage be able to go ahead if rings were not used?
d Read through the marriage vows. Summarise what these are saying in your own words.
e Why do you think that some brides do not want to say 'obey' and some do?
f Video a role play of a marriage ceremony in a church. Add narration between the different actions, explaining what is happening. You need to cover the reasons for marriage, the objections, the consent, the vows, the ring(s), the proclamation and the blessing.

▲ A Russian Orthodox wedding service, in which wedding crowns are used.

THE MEANING OF MARRIAGE

A special union

Roman Catholics, Orthodox and Anglicans call marriage a sacrament. All Christians think that a special blessing is given. The couple are spiritually joined together. This idea comes from the story in Genesis where Adam and Eve are created. 'At last, here is one of my own kind – bone taken from my bone, and flesh from my flesh.' The author goes on, 'a man leaves his father and mother and is united with his wife, and they become one' (Genesis 2:23–4, Good News Bible). Jesus also talked about the special union that God fashions between a man and his wife: 'Man must not separate, then, what God has joined together' (Mark 10:9, New International Version). The Hebrew Bible called marriage a 'seal upon the heart', and a modern Anglican prayer for the couple echoes this, and the Orthodox custom of crowning: 'Let their love for each other be a seal upon their hearts and a crown upon their heads.'

Civil and religious vows: what is the difference?

Christians believe that the difference between the vows taken in a church and those taken in a register office is that they are made before God. His name is called upon as a witness to the marriage, and his blessing is sought.

Why get married?

Christians in the past used to think that the main reason for marriage was so that the couple could have children. But marriage is now seen, by all Christians, as being about companionship first and foremost. Sexual activity is part of that deep relationship. Most couples do have children, and feel fulfilled in having them.

The Roman Catholic Church teaches that children are the fruit and fulfilment of sexual union, of the deep love between husband and wife. This may be so, but many now want to be able to plan responsibly when to have them, and how many to have. Most Churches accept artificial methods of birth control within the marriage relationship. The Roman Catholic Church only accepts natural methods, but many Catholics disagree over this.

It is interesting to compare two Service Books in the Church of England to see the changing attitudes. The seventeenth-century Book of Common Prayer has these three reasons for marriage: (1) to have children; (2) for sex; (3) for companionship. The 2000 Common Worship Book has the reasons in this order: (1) for companionship; (2) for sex; (3) to have children.

The marriage service helps the couple to feel more committed to each other psychologically, because they make a public commitment. They feel they have the support of their family and friends and the Church. They also call upon God's blessing. A verse in the Hebrew Bible says

Marriage is a gift of God in creation through which husband and wife may know the grace of God. It is given that as man and woman grow together in love and trust, they shall be united with one another in heart, body and mind, as Christ is united with his bride, the Church.

The gift of marriage brings husband and wife together in the delight and tenderness of sexual union and joyful commitment to the end of their lives. It is given as the foundation of family life in which children are (born and) nurtured and in which each member of the family, in good times and in bad, may find strength, companionship and comfort, and grow to maturity in love.

The Marriage Service: Common Worship

a Referring to the text above, write out any reasons for marriage in your own words. Which do you think are the most important?
b Why do you think that the phrase 'born and' is placed in brackets?

'a threefold cord cannot easily be broken'. In weddings, this is taken as the love of a man for a woman and the blessing of God.

Divorce

All Christians agree that marriage should be intended for life. That is the ideal. If a minister felt that a couple were not sure that they wanted to spend the rest of their lives together, he would talk them out of it. Yet not all marriages are successful. Some do break down. It is here that Christians are divided on what to do next.

- Roman Catholics do not allow divorce. They argue that since marriage is a sacrament, it is binding for life, and a couple cannot be unmarried. They can live separately, but they cannot divorce and remarry. They refer to Jesus' words in Mark 10:9 and to the view of Paul expressed in 1 Corinthians 7:10–11 where he allows separation but not divorce.
- Catholics do allow **annulment**. This is a declaration that a marriage never in fact took place, and there are strict conditions, which show that at least one of the couple did not intend to make the vows properly at the time of the wedding.

> A wife must not separate from her husband. But if she does, she must remain unmarried or else be reconciled to her husband. And a husband must not divorce his wife.
>
> *1 Corinthians 7:10–11*

- Most other Christians do allow divorce. They point to Jesus' words in Matthew 5:31–2 where he says that divorce can happen because of adultery. If one thing can break a marriage, then other things can, too, such as cruel treatment, desertion or a complete breakdown in the relationship.
- Orthodox Christians are sometimes **excommunicated** for a time after divorce (meaning that they cannot take the sacraments in church) if they were the guilty party. Then they are re-admitted after a service in which they express their sorrow over contributing to the ending of the marriage. They believe that marriage is a solemn union that should be for life, but it can break down from within.
- Some Christians feel that divorced people should not remarry because their first marriage failed. Others feel it is only humanitarian to allow people to remarry, especially if they were the innocent party. Orthodox Christians can remarry, but without the full marriage ceremony. In the Church of England either a blessing of a second marriage is allowed, once this has taken place in a register office, or a full, second marriage in church if it can be shown that the couple were the innocent parties and there is no cause for scandal.

Read the following:

- Mark 10:9
- 1 Corinthians 7:10–11
- Matthew 5:31–2

a What views are held about marriage and divorce in these passages?

b How do these verses help present-day Christians to work out what is right and wrong?

FAMILY LIFE

KEY QUESTION

What is a family and why is it important?

'The domestic church'

Christians think highly of the family and seek to encourage and protect it. Marriage and family are meant to provide a stable foundation for the bringing up of children. Pope John Paul II called the family 'the domestic church' for that is a little community where love and sharing should be uppermost, and faith in God is at the heart. Different Churches have different ways of helping the family to grow spiritually together. Families are encouraged to worship together at church and to pray at home. Some traditions, such as the Orthodox, have long-standing devotions that families take part in. They have an icon corner in their homes. The family gather around this, facing the images of Jesus, Mary and the saints. They sing chants and say prayers. At other times, festivals are partly celebrated at home, such as having Easter eggs.

What type of family?

Western Europe and the USA usually means a nuclear family when they speak of 'families'. A nuclear family is made up of two parents and their children. However, there are an increasing number of single-parent families in society. There are also extended families where grandparents or cousins, uncles or aunts might live with the parents and children. This extended

This picture is of an icon corner in a private home.

a What would this be used for?

b What Christian denomination would the family belong to?

c How might this help the family to be strong?

model is more in keeping with biblical times and its traditional culture.

There is also a sense of the Church family, beyond blood relationships. Christians are supposed to be a spiritual family. Going to worship in church should give a sense of belonging and support. People on their own can then feel they are part of a family.

Birth control

The Roman Catholic Church accepts natural methods of contraception, such as the rhythm method. This defines a woman's fertile cycle each month and these are times of the month when she is very unlikely to get pregnant. They reject artificial methods such as condoms or the pill as this is deliberately interfering in the process. Each act of sexual union should be open to the procreation of life, even if there are times of the month when this would be very unlikely. Not all Catholics follow this teaching, though, appealing to their own consciences. They feel that the well being of their family and their relationships must come first. Other Churches do accept artificial methods of contraception as a responsible form of family planning. Many reject the IUD method (e.g. the coil) or the morning after pill as these are a form of early abortion – they prevent a fertilised egg from implanting in the lining of the womb.

Abortion

The Roman Catholic Church forbids **abortion**, seeing this as a form of murder. They teach that the fertilised egg has an immortal soul from the moment of conception. For this reason, any

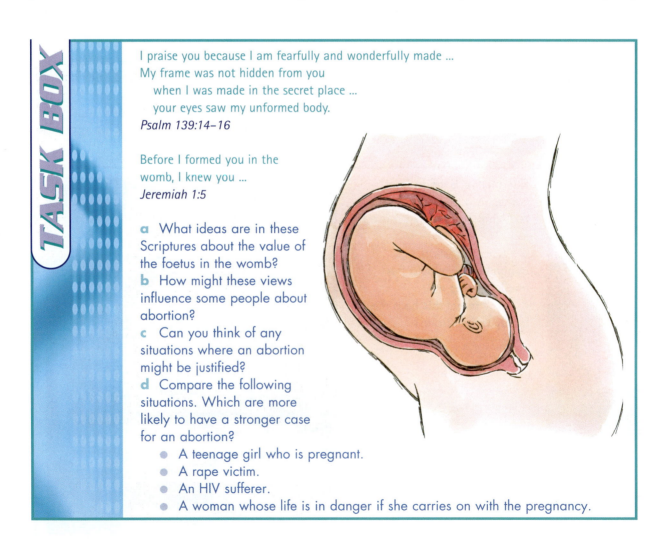

TASK BOX

I praise you because I am fearfully and wonderfully made ...
My frame was not hidden from you
    when I was made in the secret place ...
    your eyes saw my unformed body.
Psalm 139:14–16

Before I formed you in the womb, I knew you ...
Jeremiah 1:5

a What ideas are in these Scriptures about the value of the foetus in the womb?
b How might these views influence some people about abortion?
c Can you think of any situations where an abortion might be justified?
d Compare the following situations. Which are more likely to have a stronger case for an abortion?
- A teenage girl who is pregnant.
- A rape victim.
- An HIV sufferer.
- A woman whose life is in danger if she carries on with the pregnancy.

A New Approach – Christianity

technology, such as IVF treatment, that uses fertilised eggs is also rejected, as some of the eggs are wasted in the process.

Other Churches are wary of abortion, too, for a foetus has the potential to be a fully, living human being at least. There are scientific and religious debates about when a foetus becomes a living being, an individual with a personality or soul. Some trace this to the first stages of brain activity after several weeks, some even to the moment of birth itself when the child takes its first, unaided breath. However we define this, the fact is that a fertilised egg, left undisturbed, will continue to develop, stage by stage until the baby is born. The foetus is thus a sacred thing, a human being growing.

All Christians reject abortion as means of birth control. There are times when it is not so easy. A young, unmarried mother might fear that she cannot cope and support a child. Is it fair to bring it into the world? A mother with HIV might fear that her child would be born with it. A woman might find herself pregnant because she was raped – should she be forced to have the child?

These are stressful dilemmas, but some would point out that adoption would be an option. At least that way the baby would live and have a chance. The HIV case is more tricky. There are chances that the baby might not develop that condition, and even if it did, would not a short life span, being loved and cherished, be better than a termination? It is easy to make judgements when we are not in the situation.

Then there are health issues that are more cut and dried. If the mother's health is seriously at risk, and treatment is needed that will abort the pregnancy, then all Churches recognise the need to proceed with medical intervention. Even the Roman Catholic Church, for all its strictness on this matter, sees this as the lesser of two evils. The aim is not to kill the child, but to save the life of the mother.

PERSPECTIVES

At the turn of the twenty-first century, a young Anglican curate, Rev. Joanna Jepson, campaigned to have doctors prosecuted for agreeing to the abortion of a foetus that was found to have a cleft palate when scans were taken of the womb. A cleft palate used to be a serious disfigurement, but, in most cases, a simple act of surgery can correct this now. She hit the headlines with her campaign. She had been disfigured as a child, with a jaw problem that was corrected later. She also has a Down's syndrome brother. She spoke out for the rights of the unborn and for the right to life.

What made her speak out?
Do you think individual protests like this can change society?

TEST YOURSELF

1 Give an example of natural contraception.
2 Give an example of artificial contraception.
3 Why is the Roman Catholic Church opposed to artificial contraception?
4 Why are most Christians opposed to IUD methods?

FUNERALS

> ### KEY QUESTION
>
> How do funeral services help the bereaved person?

The service

Friends and relatives will gather together for the funeral service. It might open with the minister saying some words of Jesus, such as 'I am the resurrection, and I am the life; he who believes in me, though he die, yet shall he live, and whoever lives and believes in me shall never die' (John 11:25–6, New International Version).

After some singing and praying, the minister will say a few words about the deceased person, summing up the value of his or her life and how he or she will be missed; and then if the person is to be buried, as the coffin is lowered into the grave, the minister says the **committal** (these are the Anglican words): 'We have entrusted our brother/sister [Name] to God's merciful keeping, and we now commit his/her body to the ground: earth to earth, ashes to ashes, dust to dust: in sure and certain hope of the resurrection to eternal life through our Lord Jesus Christ, who died, was buried, and rose again for us. To him be glory for ever and ever.'

These are the Roman Catholic words: 'Father, into your hands we commend our brother (sister). We are confident that with all who have died in Christ he/she will be raised to life on the last day and live with Christ forever ...'

The Orthodox service has similar words, but

a What is the committal?
b Why is this a very sensitive part of the service?
c Read through the words said at this point. What do they have to say about hope and the need to let go?

adds, later on, 'May Christ give thee rest in the land of the living, and open unto thee the gates of Paradise, and make thee a citizen of his Kingdom.'

If the person is cremated, only slightly different words will be said.

In some Churches there will be a Eucharist said in memory of the dead person as a part of the service. This is called a requiem.

After the service

There will usually be a meal or a gathering afterwards for all the guests, and this will allow them time to share their sorrows and memories, as well as meet people they may not have seen for some time. More traditional cultures will hold a wake, a time of partying and mourning, with laughter mixed with tears as people celebrate the person's memory and weep together. This can sometimes go on for days. Western European society is usually more reserved, and customs around the world show very different ways of coping with bereavement. In Afro-Caribbean funerals, for example, the coffin will be open during the service. The people will walk past this, paying their last respects, kissing, looking or touching the body. The mourners will sing around the graveside while the men present fill in the grave. Flowers are poured over the grave forming a huge mound. People will then gather together for the rest of the day.

The value of the service

A funeral service helps people to face up to the loss of a friend or relative. It is a public act of saying farewell, and all the people there share in the sorrow to some degree. It is a formal 'goodbye' and it helps the process of mourning and adjusting to loss.

Christians believe in a life after death. They believe that a deceased person's body might rot away in the grave or be cremated into ashes, but their personality lives on, somehow, raised to new life by God. This is in a place that is impossible to imagine. The story of Jesus rising again helps to give them confidence in this hope. Some of the prayers and readings stress this hope; others ask for people to be comforted.

No eye has seen,
  no ear has heard,
no mind conceived
  what God has prepared for those who love him.

1 Corinthians 2:9 (Isaiah 64:4)

TASK BOX

a Plan what you think would be an ideal gathering after a funeral service.
b Why do you think that this would be appropriate?

TASK BOX

a Why do some people believe in a life after death? Think of as many reasons as you can. Talk about this in groups, if you wish.
b What do you think, personally?
c Does a belief in life after death help a mourner at a funeral service?

COMMUNITY LEADERS

> ### KEY QUESTION
>
> Why do Churches have leaders and why do they have special ways of dressing?

What are they called?

All Churches have leaders. They might have different titles and dress differently, but they perform a very similar role. In the early Church there were elders and overseers, and servers. An overseer was the senior elder over a large church. He had a group of assistants, the elders around him. They led the services, taught and presided at the Eucharist. The Greek words used were *episkopos* for the overseer, and *presbyter* for the elder. There is not always a clear distinction between the two offices in the Bible, but they came to be seen as separate, and gradually became known as bishops and priests in English. (Priest was an abbreviation of *presbyter*.)

The servers were originally known as **deacons**. They looked after the widows and orphans, made sure food was shared out, and helped to take the Eucharist to the sick. Over time, when the church grew, a bishop saw over a large area called a diocese. Each parish church or local gathering was led by a priest. Deacons assisted the priests for many years, but their role gradually fell into disuse. The Orthodox Churches kept them going, and some permanent deacons have been introduced both into the Roman Catholic and Anglican Churches. Otherwise, a person spends a year as a deacon before being ordained priest.

At the Reformation, people tried to go back to the Bible. The Bible does not always show any clear difference between overseers and elders, and many Reformed churches just had elders (sometimes called pastors, as in the Lutheran churches.) They were reacting, too, against the role of bishops in the medieval Church, who had become powerful lords of the realm with palaces and riches. The early Church bishops were simpler, more ordinary men. At first, they had no special clothes, mitres nor staffs.

Why do they do it?

Christians believe that some people have a **vocation**. This is a special calling to work as a pastor, minister or priest. Some people feel a call, or a vocation, to be a monk or a nun, too. In some Churches priests or ministers can marry; in others, they have to remain single. Priests are normally celibate (being single and abstaining from sexual relationships) in the Roman Catholic Church. This is so that they can totally dedicate themselves to their work and the people. In the Orthodox Churches, a married man can be a priest, but if you are single then you must remain celibate when ordained. Such a person is automatically part of a monastic order.

How do they dress?

Bishops, priests and deacons have dressed differently through the ages. What they might wear in a service is different from everyday life, too. There might be ceremonial robes for worship.

Some ministers might just wear ordinary clothes, like a smart suit. This would be the case in many of the Independent (Free) Churches. This is to emphasise that all believers are equal; the minister leads the services because he or she is specially trained and called, that is all. However, other Churches have ministers who dress in special robes to take a service. It might be a long, white robe called an **alb**, or a shorter one called a **surplice**. The whiteness suggests purity and life – the goodness of God. In Roman Catholic, Orthodox and some Anglican churches the minister will wear a series of colourful robes. These give a sense of grandeur and beauty to a service, as an offering to God. The main robes would be the alb; the **stole**, like a colourful scarf; and the **chasuble**, which slips over the head. The colours of the stole and chasuble will vary throughout the year, from purple, white or gold, to red and green. The chasuble may have designs on it, such as stylised doves or crosses.

> ## TEST YOURSELF
>
>
> 1 What is a *presbyter*?
> 2 What is an *episkopos*?
> 3 What is a deacon?
> 4 Who has pastors?

▲ A minister wearing an alb (a white robe), chasuble and stole (the scarf). At what time of year might green be worn?

In everyday life, there might be some sort of distinctive uniform. In the Middle Ages, for example, priests and bishops had a tonsure, a circle of hair shaved off. The clerical collar did not become fashionable until the nineteenth century, and this evolved from a white scarf around the neck that civil servants of all types used to wear.

Free Church ministers or pastors also tend to use the clerical collar as this is a universal sign of a Christian minister now. Some very modern leaders will wear casual clothes and shun a special collar. They feel that this is archaic and want to be on a level with ordinary people. They point out that the first Christian leaders did not adopt any distinctive dress. They would have worn Roman togas. Today, the equivalent is a pair of jeans and a T-shirt!

TEST YOURSELF

1 Why do some ministers wear special robes and some do not?
2 What is an alb?
3 What is a surplice?
4 What is a stole?
5 What is a chasuble?
6 Which service would a chasuble and stole be worn for?

TASK BOX

a Why do the Independent Churches not have bishops?
b Did bishops always have a mitre and a pastoral staff?
c Where did the clerical collar develop from?
d How did the first Christian leaders dress?
e How useful do you think special collars and robes are for clergy today?
f Find out when and why the colours of the stole and chasuble vary throughout the year.

TAIZÉ: AN EXAMPLE OF A MONASTIC COMMUNITY

A monk or a nun takes vows of poverty, chastity and obedience. They live in communities, share their goods, and do not marry. They seek to live the Christian life in radical commitment, giving their all. They take visitors, counsel them and pray for them, as well as praying several times each day for the world. In the past, they would run hospitals and schools. Though this can happen, it is more rare today. Such things are looked after by the state.

An example of an ecumenical monastic community is Taizé in south-east France. This community of monks is made up of members from several different Churches and was formed after the Second World War by Roger Schutz (Brother Roger). During the war he had helped Jewish refugees in his house in the village. He had a vision of a Christian community where young people could visit to worship and discuss problems. Taizé community can be visited by members of all the Churches, all religions and by people who have no religion. Many young people camp out in the fields nearby and join in prayer, worship and discussion groups. Some might help in the kitchens, or do other odd jobs on the land. The food is simple, and the hospitality is warm and friendly. The worship contains simple songs in Latin and in other languages (mainly French, English and German). Candles blaze at the front of the church, and icons are all around it. The Easter vigil is held each Saturday evening, during which the congregation hold flickering candles. Taizé is an opportunity for young people to make friends from different countries in Europe.

▲ Saturday evening worship at Taizé.

> When the Churches are reconciled to each other, the nations will come running to her like a mother.
>
> *Brother Roger*

▲ Roger Schutz (Brother Roger), founder of Taizé community.

A New Approach – Christianity

TASK BOX

'It's of little value spending your time locked up in a monastery!'

Do you agree? Answer this by describing the work of a monastic community.

AGAPE LOVE

Paul wrote his first letter to Christians in Corinth, in Greece, because he heard that they were having problems. Some of them liked to think they were wiser than the rest and more spiritual. Some of them seemed to have spiritual gifts, such as faith healing and the ability to speak in strange languages when they praised God. Paul pointed out that all their wisdom and gifts were utterly worthless if they did not have love. Any gifts that people had were God-given to build up their community, to help each other, and not there for showing-off.

If I speak in the tongues of men and of angels, but have not love, I am only a resounding gong or a clanging cymbal. If I have the gift of prophecy and can fathom all mysteries and all knowledge, and if I

have faith that can move mountains, but have not love, I am nothing. If I give all I possess to the poor and surrender my body to the flames, but have not love, I gain nothing. Love is patient, love is kind. It does not envy, it does not boast, it is not proud. It is not rude, it is not self-seeking, it is not easily angered, it keeps no record of wrongs. Love does not delight in evil but rejoices with the truth. It always protects, always trusts, always hopes, always perseveres. Love never fails. But where there are prophecies, they will cease; where there are tongues, they will be stilled; where there is knowledge, it will pass away. For we know in part and we prophesy in part, but when perfection comes, the imperfect disappears. When I was a child, I talked like a child. I thought like a child, I reasoned like a child. When I became a man, I put childish ways behind me. Now we see but a poor reflection as in a mirror; then we shall see face to face. Now I know in part; then I shall know fully, even as I am fully known. And now these three remain: faith, hope and love. But the greatest of these is love.

1 Corinthians 13

Paul's teaching about love forms the thirteenth chapter of his letter, and it is often called the hymn to love. The word for love that he uses in Greek is ***agape***, a suffering love. It is the word used of the love Jesus showed when going to the cross. It is a love that is prepared to be hurt in the service of others, not asking for anything in return.

Paul argues that only love is eternal; all other gifts will pass away when the Kingdom comes. He is saying the same thing as Jesus in the Great Commandment (Mark 12:28–34), in his own way.

CHARITY

The old English word for *agape* type love is 'charity', a love that gives. There are many different charities today that work in the world and give people money too. Christians have charities that work in developing countries.

The Greeks had a number of different words for 'love'. St Paul writes about *agape* love.

a Describe, in your own words, what *agape* love is, and give an example.
b List some other types of love with examples.
c What types of love are shown in the pictures above?

Christian Aid works in many different areas, helping various groups and projects. Picture 1 on p127 shows the people of Banderas, in Honduras, helping to unload the first lorries of relief supplies after Hurricane Mitch devastated their region. The lorries were supported by Christian Aid.

Picture 2 shows peace and civic education drama in a camp for displaced people in Sierra Leone. It was organised by the Christian Aid-sponsored MCSL Peace and Civic Education Project.

The hands of this woman in picture 3 show skin cancer as the result of years of poisoning. Some people use old wells in Bangladesh that have ancient, deep, tubes burrowed down into the earth. Arsenic poisoning results, and this slowly hurts people, building up little by little over the years. Christian Aid supports projects that teach such people how to dig new wells and use clean water.

Find out about some examples of projects sponsored by charities such as CAFOD, Tearfund, or some other projects helped by Christian Aid.

▲ Picture 1   Relief supplies in Honduras after Hurricane Mitch.

▲ Picture 3   A woman with skin cancer in Bangladesh.

▲ Picture 2   Educational drama in a refugee camp in Sierra Leone.

WEBLINKS

The following sites will give information about the charities mentioned in this chapter:

🕷 www.christian-aid.org.uk

🕷 www.tearfund.org.uk

🕷 www.cafod.org.uk

A site dealing with weddings is
🕷 www.weddingguide.co.uk

A site dealing with the Taize community is
🕷 www.taize.fr

REMEMBER

- We all need rites of passage at different stages of life.
- Marriage is about commitment and a spiritual union.
- Some Churches allow divorce; others do not.
- Funeral services help by allowing mourners to say a final goodbye.
- Belief in life after death gives some hope at a time of loss.

---

1 Describe a Christian marriage service. [8]

2 Explain why the vows made at this service are important. [7]

3 'Parents have a responsibility to instil their beliefs into their children.'
Do you agree? Give reasons to support your answer and show that you have considered other points of view. You should refer to Christianity in your answer. [5]

4 Give an example of *agape* in action in the work of Christian Aid. [8]

5 Explain what *agape* is. [7]

6 'It's no use spending your time locked up in a monastery!'
Answer this by describing the work of a monastic community such as Taizé. [5]

Assignment

0

KEY WORDS

Apocalyptic – a style of writing that uses vivid symbols and poetry to describe the end of the world.

Apocrypha – a collection of books that were included in the Greek translation of the Old Testament.

Bible – from a Greek word meaning 'the books'.

Canon – a standard or rule. The canon of the Bible is the list of books it contains.

Conservative – people who seek to be careful – conserving tradition. They have a strong belief in the Scriptures but are open to question certain things.

Epistle – a letter.

Fundamentalist – someone who believes that everything in the Bible should be taken as the absolute Word of God.

Gospel – a 'good news' book about the life of Jesus.

Liberal – someone who is much freer in his or her interpretation of the Bible, questioning many things.

Prophecy – a word from God for the present or the future.

Servant – a mysterious figure in the Hebrew Bible who will suffer and die for the sins of humanity.

Testament – a binding promise. The Old Testament contained the Law and the promise that God would be with Israel. The New Testament contains the promise that God forgives and accepts us through Jesus' death on the cross.

KEY QUESTION

What is in the Bible?

WHY USE THE BIBLE?

The **Bible** is a collection of different books. The word 'Bible' means 'books'. Most of the books form the Hebrew Bible (or Old Testament to Christians). Then there is the New Testament, dealing with the story of Jesus and the first Christians.

Christians use the Bible when they pray or seek God. They believe that its words can come alive and speak with God's voice. They call the Bible 'the Word of God', though there are different ways of understanding this.

The Bible is used for teaching and for preaching, too. People can understand their faith better and there are many guidelines for living.

In some ways, the Bible is like a Highway Code for Life. Christians follow the various commandments, the teaching of Jesus and the advice of the apostles. It is also a living book for them, don't forget. They believe that God somehow speaks through this.

The Bible contains many stories about people through the ages. Underlying it is one big story of God's plan for the world. God created life and called people to follow him. He gave a special

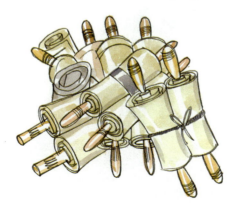

▲ People might use the Bible in private prayer or to preach from.

calling to the Hebrews, and Moses gave them the Ten Commandments. After many years of sending prophets and kings, Jesus was born. God entered the story himself, according to Christian belief. Jesus died to forgive sins, and rose again. The Bible promises that everything will end in glory, with the love of God winning over evil.

DIFFERENT BIBLES?

The Bible (also known as Scripture or the Scriptures) is the holy book of Christians. It has been translated into many different languages. It was originally written in Hebrew, Aramaic and Greek. The first official translation into English was in 1539. Before this, Bibles were written in Latin in England.

Some Bibles look very sombre, in black bindings and with old English words. But there are also many more modern translations, such as the New International Version, the Good News Bible or the Jerusalem Bible (the Roman Catholic version). All of these try to put the Bible words into modern English so that it is easier to understand. Compare these two passages, for example, from John 6:47–51. Jesus is the speaker:

▲ The Bible story – the creation; the Law; Jesus.

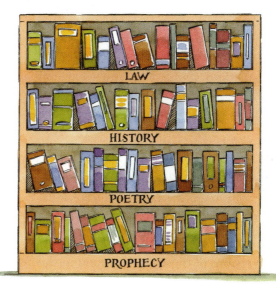

▲ **The Bible is like a library of books in one cover.**

THE HEBREW BIBLE (THE OLD TESTAMENT)

KEY QUESTION

What is in the Hebrew Bible?

Christians value the Old Testament because it was the book of the Jewish ancestors of Jesus and they interpret many of the prophecies about a coming deliverer, the Messiah, as being about Jesus. (Jewish people do not accept this, of course.)

Most English versions have 39 separate books:

- 5 law books
- 12 history books
- 5 poetry books
- 17 prophetic books (though these also contain much poetry)

The Jews divide these books into three sections: the Law, the Prophets and the Writings.

The Law

The Law (*Torah* in Hebrew) is the most important section for the Jews; it contains 613 laws. The first five books of the Bible form the Torah (Genesis, Exodus, Leviticus, Numbers and Deuteronomy). They contain many different types of laws, as well as stories about the ancestors of the Jews, like Abraham:

- There are laws for punishments, rights of slaves, repaying debts, protecting the poor, religious worship and sacrifice, for example, and even for animals that can and cannot be eaten (see Leviticus 11 and Exodus 34:26).
- The Ten Commandments are to be found in the Torah (Exodus 20:2–17).
- Orthodox Jews believe that the whole of the Law came from God, being dictated to Moses on Mount Sinai, and they try to keep as many of the laws as possible.
- Reform Jews think parts of the Law came from Moses and other laws were added later. They believe that some of the laws were relevant for their time but are now outdated, though there are general laws, such as love for

your neighbour and the worship of one God only, which are true for all ages.

■ There is the ethical law – what is right for all time. There is also the ritual law – rules and regulations about dress and what animals to eat that were more relevant to the people of the time.

Christians believe that Jesus set most of the ritual laws aside. They also believe that Jesus gave new laws, in the New Testament, and that these completed the Law God gave to Moses.

The Ten Commandments

Two versions of these can be found in the Torah. One set is in Exodus 20:2–17; the other is in Deuteronomy 5:6–21. These were originally written on two stone tablets, which were kept in the Ark of the Covenant, the decorated box that the Hebrews carried along with them. These are the heart of the Torah. They cover how to worship God and how to treat other people. There are four religious laws concerning God and six social laws concerning other people. The Hebrews were called together and told to follow these commandments out of gratitude for God

rescuing them from slavery. They were to be his special people but he expected them to live in a certain way.

The prophets

The prophets rarely foretold the future. They were *forthtellers* rather than *foretellers*. They believed they had a message from God for their times, challenging or encouraging the world they lived in. Amos, for example, in the eighth century BCE, reminded people of God's justice and challenged them to turn from their sins. He criticised the false, hypocritical religion of his day because it kept the rich *rich* and the poor *poor*.

The words of the prophets contained great insights and morals that Christians believe all ages can learn from. In a general way they did speak of the future: they spoke of the coming Messiah and of an age of peace when all would know God:

TASK BOX

a Which part of the Hebrew Bible is being read from?
b Why is this especially holy for Jews?
c What famous list of commandments can be found in this? Give one example of them.
d Give the Bible references where you would find this list (book, chapter and verses).
e Which of the ten laws are religious and which are social?
f Write the commandments out in your own words.

The wolf will live with the lamb,
the leopard will lie down with the goat,
the calf and the lion and the yearling together;
and a little child will lead them.
The cow will feed with the bear,
their young will lie down together,
and the lion will eat straw like the ox.
The infant will play near the hole of the cobra,
and the young child put his hand into the viper's nest.
They will neither harm nor destroy
on all my holy mountain,
for the earth will be full of the knowledge of the Lord
as the waters cover the sea.

Isaiah 11:6–9

Isaiah also contains a moving passage about the Servant of God who is rejected by the people and suffers for their sins. For Christians, Jesus is the Servant who went to his death on the cross. Jewish people, however, think the Servant is anyone who tries to do what is right and who is badly treated by other people. 'The Servant' for most of them is a cipher, a symbol. They see their own race in the Servant, often persecuted and slandered in history:

We all, like sheep, have gone astray,
each of us has turned to his own way;
and the LORD has laid on him
the iniquity of us all.

He was oppressed and afflicted,
yet he did not open his mouth;
he was led like a lamb to the slaughter,
and as a sheep before her shearers is silent,
so he did not open his mouth.
By oppression and judgment he was taken away.
And who can speak of his descendants?
For he was cut off from the land of the living;
for the transgression of my people he was stricken.

Isaiah 53:6–8

Other prophecies, such as Isaiah 7:14 and Daniel 7:13–14, are seen as relating to Jesus by Christians.

The prophets also predicted more local events. For example, Jeremiah predicted that Babylon, 'a foe from the north', would descend upon Judah and exile the people unless they turned from their sins. But the bulk of their teaching was forthtelling rather than foretelling.

TEST YOURSELF

1 What did a prophet do?
2 What is forthtelling?
3 Give an example of forthtelling from the prophets.
4 What is foretelling?
5 Find an example of foretelling from the prophets.

The writings

There are various types of poetry books in this section, such as the Psalms. These are prayers and hymns of praise, some by King David, with moving imagery such as these lines:

As the deer pants for streams of water,
so my soul pants for you, O God.
My soul thirsts for God, for the living God.
When can I go and meet with God?
Psalm 42:1–2

The book of Job is about an innocent man who suffers, and Proverbs is a series of wise sayings. There is even a collection of love poems, the 'Song of Songs', and a book about an ancient prophet, Daniel, which has vivid poetry that tells of the coming Kingdom of God.

Christians value these books for their insights about God. The Psalms are recited in Christian worship regularly.

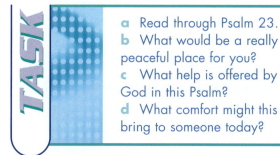

TASK

a Read through Psalm 23.
b What would be a really peaceful place for you?
c What help is offered by God in this Psalm?
d What comfort might this bring to someone today?

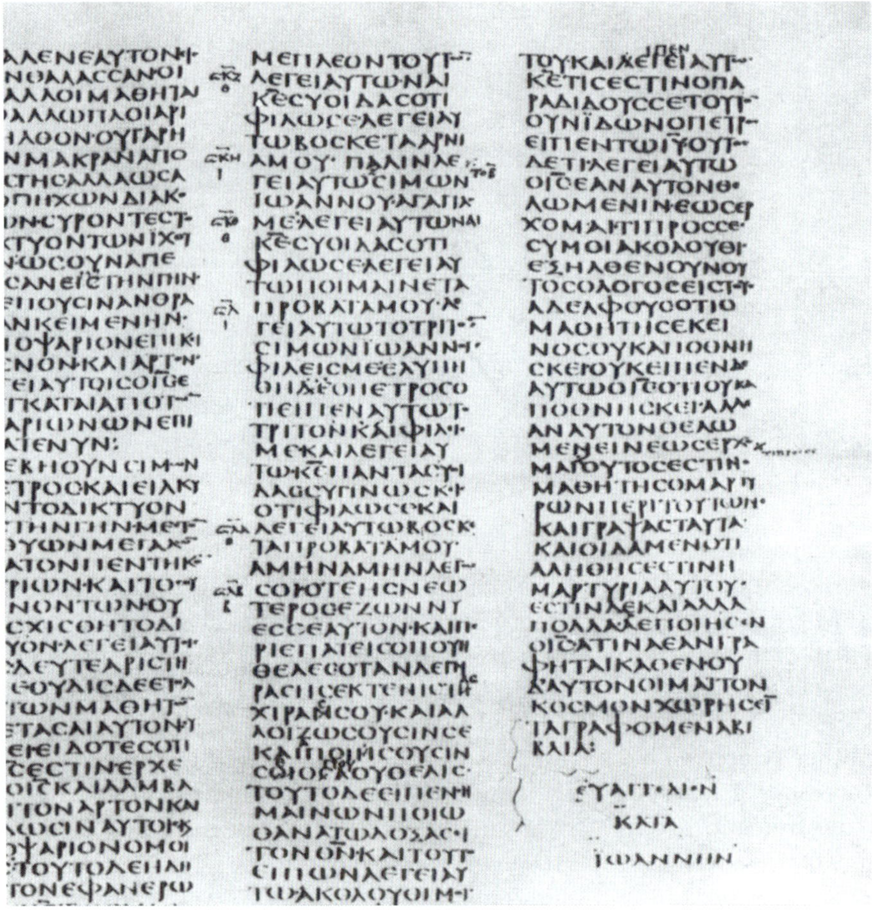

The books about Jesus

The books about Jesus are called **Gospels**. They tell the story of the main events in the life of Jesus, and contain his teaching. They are named after their traditional authors, Matthew, Mark, Luke and John. The word *gospel* means 'good news' and the idea is that the books are about the good news of the coming of Jesus and of his resurrection from the dead. The Gospels largely ignore the childhood of Jesus and are mainly concerned with the last few years of his life when he became a public preacher. They are even more interested in the last week of his life – Holy Week and his journey to the cross.

▲ Part of the New Testament written in Greek, from the fourth-century Codex Sinaiticus.

KEY QUESTION

What is in the New Testament?

The New Testament contains the writings of the early Christians, and once these had been written, the Church placed them alongside the Hebrew Bible to form the complete Christian Bible known today. The New Testament contains 27 different books:

- 4 books about Jesus
- 1 book about the first Christians
- 21 letters
- 1 prophetic book.

The book about the early Christians

The Acts of the Apostles is about the beginning of the Church, when the apostles rallied together after Jesus' death and spread the belief in his resurrection. It concentrates mainly on the exploits of Peter and Paul and finishes when Paul is awaiting trial in Rome.

The letters

Most of the New Testament is composed of **epistles**, or letters. This sounds strange at first, but there is a good reason. Most of these letters were written by Paul and his disciples, with two said to have been written by Peter, three by John (but which John – the apostle, or a later disciple?), one by James and one by Jude. These

a List the four Gospels.

b What does 'Gospel' mean?

c Why do you think that there are four accounts?

d Invent an incident and write four reports from four different people. How might these be similar and different?

e Should we expect the four Gospels to be identical to each other?

The earliest known fragment of the Gospel of John. This was found in the sands of Egypt and dates from about 110–130CE

Christian leaders wrote to gatherings of believers to give them advice and encouragement. Usually, they wrote to churches they had founded and for which they felt a special responsibility. '1 Corinthians', for example, thus means, 'The first letter that Paul wrote to the Christians in the city of Corinth'. Some of the letters are very short, like Philemon, and others are much longer, like Romans.

These letters give us an insight into the beliefs and concerns of the first Christians and, just as people found them helpful then, so too do modern Christians. They are full of spiritual insights.

to earth in victory. Most Christians accept it as poetry, and do not take it literally word for word.

Evil powers are symbolised as beasts that rise from the sea to torment the human race, and Christ returns on the clouds, in glory, to slay the beast and set the people free. It is a poetic way of talking about the final victory of good over evil. Christians debate, though, which parts of it should be understood literally and which are to be taken as symbolic.

Revelation contains a vision of the risen Christ.

TEST YOURSELF

1 What is covered in the Acts of the Apostles?

2 Why are so many letters contained in the New Testament?

3 Which apostles wrote letters?

The visionary book

The book of Revelation is a weird and wonderful work written towards the end of the first century CE. It has a series of visions, and is full of symbols and strange events. It uses a style known as apocalytptic. Its theme is that good will eventually win over evil, and that Christ is going to return

I turned round to see the voice that was speaking to me. And when I turned I saw seven golden lampstands, and among the lampstands was someone 'like a son of man', dressed in a robe reaching down to his feet and with a golden sash round his chest. His head and hair were white like wool, as white as snow, and his eyes were like blazing fire. His feet were like bronze glowing in a furnace, and his voice was like the sound of rushing waters. In his right hand he held seven stars, and out of his mouth came a sharp double-edged sword. His face was like the sun shining in all its brilliance.

When I saw him, I fell at his feet as though dead. Then he placed his right hand on me and said: 'Do not be afraid. I am the First and the Last. I am the Living One; I was dead, and behold I am alive for ever and ever! And I hold the keys of death and Hades.

Revelation 1:12–18

TASK BOX

a What kind of symbols are used to represent good and evil in Revelation?

b Why do you think symbols are used?

c Read through the passage about the risen Christ. How does this make the reader feel? What symbols are used here?

d Compare this with the Servant passage in Isaiah 53. What different ideas, images and feelings are there in this?

THE TESTAMENTS

KEY QUESTION

Why are the two sections of the Bible known as 'Testaments'?

The two parts of the Bible are called Testaments because both Jews and Christians believe that God has made a special agreement with humankind. ('**Testament**' here means agreement or promise. Another word for it is a 'covenant'.) In the Old Testament God promised to guide the Jews and reveal his laws to them. In the New Testament, Christians believe that God has shown how much he loves all people through Jesus dying on the cross, and promises them life after death.

The Bible, therefore, is a collection of different books, written at different times by different authors. It did not fall out of the sky one day, and was not written by just one person! It is like a library of religious books, some by Jews, some by Christians. In fact, the word Bible comes from the Greek word *biblia* meaning 'the books'. They would have been copied out on individual scrolls before the book format was invented.

The canon

Canon is a Greek word that meant 'a measuring rod'. It then came to mean a list of books accepted as genuine. The canon of the Bible means the correct list of books that are in it. The canon of the Old Testament has been fixed as the books of the Law, of the Prophets and the Writings, by the time of Jesus. The canon of the New Testament was finally settled by about 200 CE. Most of the books were agreed before this date, however. In order to be included, books had to be widely read by Christians, had to be considered helpful, and either had to be written by one of the apostles or thought to be faithful to their teachings.

The Apocrypha

There is also a collection of writings that some Bibles include with the Old Testament, and that other Bibles print as a separate section in between the Old Testament and the New Testament. They are called **Apocrypha**, which means 'hidden (books)', because they are disputed. Some think they should not be in the canon.

There are seven writings – some are lengthy books, some short letters or extracts. They were included in the Greek translation of the Old Testament that was made in the ancient world, but not in the Hebrew canon. The early Christians used the Greek Old Testament widely and carried on using the extra writings in their Bible. In the fourth century, the Christian scholar Jerome called these extra writings the Apocrypha and doubted whether they should be of the same standing as the rest of the Bible. He thought the events in them were more doubtful. Protestant Christians do not print the books as part of their Bible, but Roman Catholics still do, as in the modern Jerusalem Bible.

The books of the Apocrypha were composed between 300 BCE and 100 CE. The writings contain stories of the Jewish ancestors, Tobit and Judith and the stories of the Maccabees, Jewish freedom fighters in the century before Jesus, as well as many wise sayings.

TEST YOURSELF

1 What does 'testament' mean?
2 What are the two testaments of the Bible based upon?
3 What is meant by the canon of Scripture?
4 What is the Apocrypha?

THE BIBLE IN CHRISTIAN LIFE AND WORSHIP

The Bible is used in a variety of ways in Christian life and worship. It is not just an ancient book, an old classic, read out of interest, as people might read the works of Julius Caesar or the ancient Greek writers. Christians read it not only to try to find out more about their faith, but also to try to hear the voice of God within them. It is a living book, to them.

In Church

In church services, lessons from the Bible will be read, and the congregation will listen. A saying, a verse, a phrase might jump out at them and suggest an answer to a problem, or help to guide them in making a decision. Or perhaps this will click into place during the sermon, when the preacher might comment on various aspects of the passages that are read out. In some churches, the Gospels will be carried with great respect, and all will stand when they are read out. Perhaps candles will be carried alongside these to symbolise Jesus as the Light of the World. This is to show that the stories and words of Jesus stand at the centre of the Bible, the most important and most holy part.

In small groups

The Bible is also studied in small groups who meet in church or in someone's home. The minister, or some other member of the congregation, will read through some passages, think about them, look them up in a commentary written by experts, and will then lead the group in study and discussion. This will give people the opportunity of asking questions and raising doubts, an opportunity they do not have in a formal church service.

The Bible studies might be applied to problems of everyday life, such as finding a goal in life, coping with depression or family life. Or social problems might be focused on, like racism, war or unemployment. In this way, Christians may come to a deeper understanding of their faith and its application to life.

Personal use

The Bible will also be used for personal study or meditation. Christians might set aside a few minutes each day for prayer and study. They might just open the Bible at random, or work through a particular book, or use Bible reading notes to guide them through passages and comment on them. One young person commented that this was like cuddling a favourite teddy bear when alone or needing comfort. The love of God felt through the Bible can bring peace and calm.

Meditation

A particular passage might be read through slowly, several times, so that its meaning sinks in. After doing this for some time people will think about what they have been reading and perhaps say a prayer. This is a way of using the Bible in meditation. They hope to sense the inner guidance of God through reading the words of Scripture. Some words will come alive for them, and they might carry these over into their prayers, dwelling upon them.

MAKING SENSE OF THE BIBLE

> ### KEY QUESTION
> How should we understand the Bible?

The Bible, for all Christians, is in some way the Word of God as well as a collection of human words. They hope to sense the voice of God within them as they read it. Yet there are different ways of understanding this:

a What is happening here?

b What does this tell us about how Christians feel about this section of the Bible?

c Why are candles also carried around?

d Try a simple Gospel meditation. Read through Mark 4:35–41. Close your eyes and relax. Breathe a little slower and deeper than usual. Start to imagine the scene. You are someone in the boat when the storm breaks. Run through the actions in your mind. Listen to what is said and done – this might be like a waking dream for you.

e How would you have felt if you were one of the people in the boat?

- Some think the Bible is the direct Word of God, passed down through the writers as if they were secretaries taking notes from a heavenly voice. Everything in it is factually true, and most things should be taken word for word, as they are written. *The Bible is the Word of God, word for word.*

- Some think that the Word of God came to the writers, but their own personalities and writing styles were included. They interpreted the Word that came to them: they were not just secretaries. *The Bible is the Word of God interpreted, or filtered through human beings.*

- Some take this further, and argue that the writers were human beings capable of making mistakes, and were influenced by ideas around them at the time (such as seeing the world as flat). The Bible witnesses to, or contains, the Word of God, but is not directly the Word itself. *The Bible is the Word of God interpreted – and sometimes wrongly.*

So, opinions vary amongst Christians, and not all Christians accept everything in the Bible as being true.

These three basic attitudes need to be explored further. The three opinions can be summed up as those of the **fundamentalist**, the **conservative** and the **liberal** (not in any political sense!).

The fundamentalist

The word comes from 'fundamentals', a belief in basic truths that are written down. The Bible is usually taken literally, word for word.

These Christians think that the Bible is free from *all* error because it is not the words of men, but the Word of God. If passages seem to contradict themselves in the Bible, then these can and must be explained away. In the stories of the resurrection, for example, John's Gospel has Mary Magdalene going to the tomb first, then Peter. Both found it empty but, later on Mary Magdalene was the first to see the risen Christ. Matthew, Mark and Luke have a group of women going to the tomb first, and in Matthew the first appearance of the risen Christ is to the women as they are running back to tell Peter and the others. Fundamentalists would argue that John had simply not mentioned the other women, but knew they were there.

Again, if the Bible seems to contradict science, then are scientists wrong? A case in point is with evolution. Fundamentalists believe in a six-day creation and that Adam and Eve were the first people. They spend much time and energy arguing against evolutionary theories. (Some see the six 'days' as six 'eras', however.) Humans, they say, did not evolve but were specially created by God.

The conservative

The word comes from 'conserve', to guard certain traditions and ideas.

The conservative Christian believes that something of the personality of the writers came through in the Bible; it is not directly or entirely the Word of God. Therefore, they do not feel that the Bible teaches science. Instead, it is a book about faith and knowledge of God: it is not intended to be a scientific textbook. Hence there is no difficulty in accepting some form of evolution, and seeing the six-day creation story as a poem, which says why the world was created, but not how. It is not literally true, but is spiritually true.

Conservative believers do feel that there are a number of truths that were inspired by God in the Bible, though, such as that God guides the world, spoke through the prophets, that he came in Jesus, born of a virgin, worked miracles, died for people's sins and rose from the dead. They are not too concerned about trying to make various contradictory stories match one another, such as in the details of the resurrection story. They accept that different writers may have heard different versions of the same story, but the writers are all saying that the resurrection happened, and that is the important thing.

The liberal

The word comes from 'liberty', freedom of thought and expression.

The liberal Christian feels that the Bible writers were inspired like any great writer is, such as Shakespeare. They have insights into human life that others do not have, and they are able to put these into words. The Bible writers were also thought to have had deep insights about God that can help others to know what God is like and find their way to him. The writers might have had an experience of God, and they tried to put this into words, but they could make mistakes. For example, they thought as they had been taught, and held the same ideas about science that other people in the ancient world had.

Liberals feel that many passages of the Bible are symbolic poetry and should not be taken word for word. Liberals have a problem believing anything that cannot be rationally explained. They tend to write the supernatural out of the stories. For example, some liberals think that all the miracle stories in the Gospels are symbolic of great truths in the teaching of Jesus, but that they did not actually happen (thus, the healing of a blind man means that Jesus teaches people how to see spiritual things in life: he opens people's eyes, as it were). Other liberals feel that even if some of the healing stories did actually happen, then the nature miracles, such as walking on water, are symbolic stories. Liberals do not believe that the virgin birth happened; instead, they see it as a story with a meaning – God was in Jesus more than in any other man. Also, they do not accept the story of the empty tomb, but think that Jesus rose again only spiritually.

Liberal Christians try to find the kernel of truth in the Bible stories, which they think often contain errors or symbols that need to be understood properly.

a List the key ideas a fundamentalist, a conservative and a liberal christian have about the Bible?

b How would you sum up the differences between the three points of view?

A significant group of Christians are fundamentalist, particularly in the United States. They fear that once you question one thing in the Bible, you will not know where to stop. Other Christians fear that if you do accept all that the Bible says, it will mean believing in things that are impossible to believe any more, like the six-day creation. They think it is better to take what seems good and sensible, and to leave a question mark over other things.

PERSPECTIVES

The divinely revealed realities, which are contained and presented in the text of sacred Scripture have been written down under the inspiration of the Holy Spirit. ... God inspired the human authors of the sacred books. To compose the sacred books, God chose certain men who, all the while he employed them in this task, made full use of their own faculties and powers so that they consigned to writing whatever he wanted written, and no more.
Catechism of the Catholic Church

This presents a conservative view of Scripture. Why?

In its extreme form the dogma of the Infallibility of Scripture should mean that all parts of the Canon are directly and equally inspired by God, so that its every statement, whether concerning the mysteries of the divine being, the processes of nature, or the facts of history, past or future, should be exactly and literally true ...
C H Dodd, The Authority of the Bible

How does Dodd define the fundamentalist use of the Bible, here? Dodd was a liberal scholar, but one with a strong sense of God's reality. He argued that we can find God's presence in the Scriptures despite all the questions of history and interpretation.

But supposing we have found that by approaching the Bible in that 'child-like' spirit of openness and sincerity our outlook on life has been altered, our experience deepened, and our sense of God made stronger, then the beliefs enunciated by the writers to whom we owe this will carry weight with us.
C H Dodd, The Authority of the Bible

How does he show here that the Bible can be something other than a textbook or a book of knowledge?

It might be useful to look at a few examples from the Bible to compare and contrast the fundamentalist, conservative and liberal viewpoints. The passages to be studied will be:

- Joshua and the walls of Jericho (Old Testament: Joshua 6)
- the feeding of the five thousand (New Testament: Mark 6:33–44; Matthew 14:13–21; Luke 9:10–17; John 6:1–14)
- the healing of a blind man (New Testament: John 9).

JOSHUA AND JERICHO

Joshua leads the Hebrews against the Canaanite city of Jericho. God tells him to get the Hebrews to march round it once a day for six days and on the seventh day they are to march round it again, with the priests blowing trumpets at the front, and the men giving a loud shout. They do this, the walls collapse, and they rush in and kill everyone, men, women, young and old, and all the cattle they find. They set fire to the city and do not take any loot from it. Only a prostitute, Rahab, is spared, because she had allowed two Hebrew spies into her house earlier.

Below are three opinions that (1) want to keep the story as it is, (2) partly chip away at it,

and interpret it and (3) largely dismiss it as barbaric and irrelevant to Christian faith today.

The fundamentalist

It happened just as it says it did. The killing of the inhabitants does sound savage, but this was a long time before Jesus when God was working more from a position of justice and righteousness than mercy. The inhabitants had opposed the Hebrews, the people of God. Judgement came upon them. How the walls fell down is debatable – it might have been an earthquake that coincided with the seventh blast of the trumpet, or a supernatural intervention by God. There is evidence of collapsed walls and a raid on the city from archaeology. The story teaches us to have faith in God's power in the face of overwhelming odds.

The conservative

This is based upon a great deal of truth. The walls came tumbling down and this was probably the result of an earthquake. Why look for a supernatural event when one is not needed? The killing of the people was savage, and was the way of the Hebrews then. It cannot be justified spiritually. They were a primitive people and much more about the true nature of God had yet to be revealed. The conservative would agree with the spiritual lessons seen in the story by the fundamentalist.

The liberal

This might not have happened like this at all. It might be exaggerated and it is savage. The Hebrews were very primitive. There might have been an earthquake, but the evidence for this is difficult to date. Some archaeologists date this earthquake to a much earlier time – before the Hebrews were there. It is a folk tale, with very little moral or spiritual value.

▲ One level of ancient Jericho unearthed by archaeologists, showing collapsed walls and scorching. This suggests the city had been invaded.

TASK BOX

a From the text on p141, which Christian thinks that something happened in reality?
b What do you think are the main differences here between fundamentalists, conservatives and liberals?
c What do you think about this story?

THE FEEDING OF THE FIVE THOUSAND

All four Gospels contain the same basic story: a crowd of people follow Jesus, it gets late and they are hungry. Jesus blesses five loaves and two fish, and shares them round with the crowd of about 5,000 people. Everyone eats their fill, and there are 12 baskets full of leftovers. John's Gospel adds the detail that the disciples got the loaves and fish from a young boy in the crowd.

The following represent three opinions of this story: it (1) was a literal, supernatural event, (2) might have been a supernatural miracle or Jesus setting a good example, and (3) was Jesus setting a good example.

The fundamentalist

It was a miracle, a supernatural event, and it has been recorded in God's Word. It was a sign that Jesus was the Messiah – he multiplied the food and satisfied everyone's need. The story can be given a spiritual meaning, too: if we come to Jesus with what little we have, then it can increase our faith and our joy beyond all expectations.

The conservative

All four Gospels record it, and so it is very likely to have happened. How did it happen? Perhaps it was a supernatural event. Maybe the sharing of a little bit of food by some shamed the rest into producing what little they had, and when they all shared there was more than enough. We can also give it a spiritual meaning – Jesus increases our faith, if we come to him.

The liberal

This story does not involve a miracle at all in the usual sense. None of the Gospels actually or clearly claims that Jesus miraculously multiplied the food – that's what people read into it. They just say Jesus blessed the loaves and the fish, and then they all ate their fill. Perhaps Jesus set a good example by sharing out the food he had, and this made everyone else share their food, too, so there was enough for everyone! The real miracle is that Jesus stopped people being selfish and made them share with one another.

TASK BOX

a All three believe that something really happened. Can you explain what they think happened?
b What are the differences between the fundamentalists, conservatives and liberals?
c What do you think about this story?

THE HEALING OF THE BLIND MAN

▲ Miles Hilton-Barber with his specially adapted microlight aircraft. The 54-year-old, who has been blind for 20 years, launched his bid to become the first sightless person to fly across the English Channel in a microlight.

Jesus cures a blind beggar by touching his eyes with spittle and mud, and sending him to wash in the pool of Siloam. The Pharisees interrogate the man and his family, demanding to know if he is telling the truth, and if he had ever really been blind at all. The man insists that he had been blind from birth, and that he can see now. Later, Jesus warns some Pharisees that it is they who are really blind, because they will not allow him to help them to see spiritually.

Below are three opinions: (1) a literal miracle that also has a spiritual meaning, (2) a supernatural healing but the inner meaning is perhaps even more important, and (3) doubt about an actual healing, but the inner meaning is what really counts.

The fundamentalist

If it is in one of the Gospels, then it must have happened exactly as it says. Jesus had the power to heal, which was a sign that he was the Messiah. The story also reminds us that Jesus can cure our spiritual blindness, too.

The conservative

There is only one account of this story in the Gospels, but there are similar stories of blind people being healed, so it is likely that this happened. Jesus had power to heal, probably by using forces of nature that we do not understand. It also has a spiritual meaning, but this is secondary to the fact that it happened and that Jesus showed his power.

The liberal

Jesus might have used paranormal powers, but that is not really important. The inner meaning of the story matters most. It is a parable, a story with a meaning, saying that we are all spiritually blind because of our selfishness, and we are influenced to be like this from birth. Jesus can change all that; he makes you see things in a new way. That's the real miracle, that our self-centred nature can be opened up to God and other people.

TASK BOX

a What do all three groups believe about this story?

b Do fundamentalists and conservatives differ at all, here?

c What might blindness symbolise in stories, art and poetry?

d What do you think of this story?

e Work out a role play between some sceptics and a couple of believers. They are arguing about science and creation. One believer is a fundamentalist and one is a conservative.

f Create a Bible Box as a class. Make a rolled-up paper scroll using craft sticks or lollipop sticks for each book of the Bible – Old and New Testaments. Label each one and place these in a box.

WEBLINKS

Two useful sites to look at resources to study the Bible are:

🕷 www.biblesociety.org.uk
🕷 www.wycliffe.org.uk

REMEMBER

- The Bible is a library of books written at different times.
- The Bible is in two sections, Old and New Testaments.
- The New Testament covers less than a century, and the four Gospels are about Jesus.
- The Bible can be read devotionally to find spiritual guidance and peace.
- There are various ways of understanding how the Bible can be the Word of God as well as the word of human beings.

Assignment

1 Describe how Christians might use the Old Testament to show the significance of Jesus. [8]

2 Explain how and why Christians might show respect for the Bible in day-to-day living. [7]

3 'Christians should take more notice of the New Testament than of the Old testament.' Do you agree? Give reasons for your point of view and show that you have considered the views of others. [5]

4 What is the Old Testament? [2]

5 Explain how and why Christians might show respect for the Bible and use it in their daily lives. [5]

6 'Every word and idea in the Bible is the Word of God and must be believed without question.' Do you agree? Give reasons for your point of view and show consideration of those of others. Refer to Christian beliefs in your answer. [8]

11

KEY WORDS

Holy Sepulchre – the site believed to be the tomb where Jesus' body lay.
Pilgrimage – travelling to a holy place to pray and worship.
Sacrifice – an offering of time and effort.
St Peter's basilica – the main church in the Vatican.
The Vatican – the area of Rome where the Pope lives.

KEY QUESTION

What is pilgrimage?

Christians sometimes go to places to try to feel closer to God. There are special places of pilgrimage. Making the effort to travel to a place in order to pray, study and meditate helps people to take their faith seriously. It is also a way of stepping aside from the daily toil that becomes so commonplace, in order to spend time resting and thinking.

A **pilgrimage** involves travelling, but a pilgrim is more than a tourist. A tourist travels for pleasure and curiosity; a pilgrim travels to pray and worship.

Life is like a pilgrimage as people move through time from birth to death. We move along, and learn new things on the way. Going on a religious pilgrimage helps some people in their spiritual life. The great religions of the world all have places of pilgrimage. Hindus, for example, go to the sacred River Ganges. Muslims visit Mecca, their holy city. Christians visit places in the Holy Land where Jesus lived and preached, or famous shrines where saints are buried, or where people say the Virgin Mary has appeared.

▲ **Mont Saint Michel in Normandy. This ancient monastery attracts many French pilgrims. Legend has it that it was built on the orders of the Archangel Michael.**

Going on a pilgrimage benefits religious people in three ways:

1 It helps in their search for God; they often feel closer to God and more involved with him on the pilgrimage.
2 It helps people to be more aware of the passing away of their life, of their limited time on earth. It sets them thinking and helps them to work out a sense of priorities.
3 It is making an effort, and this helps them to have a disciplined spiritual life. People feel they are getting up and doing something to draw closer to God. It involves a **sacrifice** – giving up some comfort and offering up the time in prayer.

Christian places of pilgrimage have special connections with great figures or events in the Christian faith, and Christians believe that these places have a special feel about them, an awe, a special holiness that comes from being used and prayed in for centuries. For generations, pilgrims have treated these places with respect as holy places. Many pilgrims feel that something of this rubs off on them during their stay there. Besides this holy use over the ages, some believers think that God gave a special blessing to the place. He is pleased to dwell there in a deeper way than everyday life. These things are mysteries.

THE STORY OF TWO PILGRIMS

One elderly lady was on a pilgrimage to the Holy Land. She felt deeply moved as she visited places connected with the life of Jesus: they brought home to her how real a person he had been in history. In the Church of the Holy Sepulchre, where Jesus' tomb is thought to lie, she knelt down in prayer, tears streaming down her cheeks. She felt the suffering and rejection Jesus must have gone through and the mystery of the resurrection seemed all around her – somehow, he was alive.

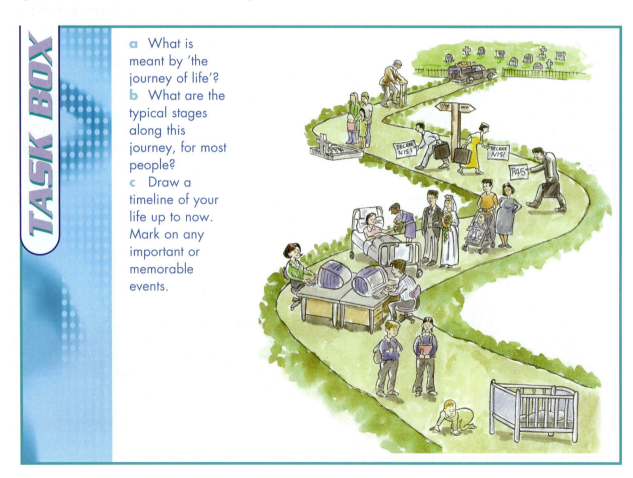

TASK BOX

a What is meant by 'the journey of life'?
b What are the typical stages along this journey, for most people?
c Draw a timeline of your life up to now. Mark on any important or memorable events.

A New Approach – Christianity

Her priest was with her, and a group of others. He had not felt anything in particular on the visit, but he knelt alongside her in the church and prayed too. He was moved when he saw her tears and her faith, and he marvelled at the fact that he had had to come all those miles to see that example of devotion.

TEST YOURSELF

1 What is the difference between a pilgrim and a tourist?
2 Why do Christians go on pilgrimage?
3 What do they seek?

'Come, follow me', Jesus said ...

Mark 1:1

BETHLEHEM: THE CHURCH OF THE NATIVITY

Bethlehem boasts the Church of the Nativity. This is the traditional site of the birth of Jesus. Although rebuilt in the sixth century, much of the original church survives. The Church of the Nativity was built by Emperor Constantine at the urging of his mother, Helena. He became the first Roman emperor to convert to Christianity, in the fourth century. But the site was regarded as holy for some time before that. Early in the second century, Emperor Hadrian built a shrine to a Roman god on it to discourage the Christians, and a Christian writer, Justin Martyr, in the second century, mentions the site as that of Jesus' birth. In 614 the Persians invaded Palestine and destroyed many churches, but the Church of the Nativity was spared, some say because the mosaic over the entrance shows the three wise men wearing Persian dress.

Various Churches have altars in the Church of the Nativity, including the Orthodox, Roman Catholic and some smaller Eastern Churches – the Armenians and the Copts. A golden star shape shows the traditional site of the birth of Jesus. Many pilgrims have knelt and prayed here.

NAZARETH

Nazareth was where Jesus grew up, and where he worked until becoming a preacher. There are two Christian sites of interest: the Basilica of the Annunciation and the Greek Orthodox Church of St Gabriel. Both claim to be the site of the Annunciation – the time when the angel Gabriel appeared to the Virgin Mary, announcing that she was going to have a child. The Basilica is modern but it stands on the site of earlier churches that were built around the cave-dwelling believed by some to have been Mary's house. Inside the Orthodox church is a well at which another tradition claims Gabriel appeared to Mary.

JERUSALEM: THE CHURCH OF THE HOLY SEPULCHRE

A shrine has existed on the spot of the Church of the Holy Sepulchre from early in the Christian period. Emperor Hadrian built a temple to a Roman goddess there in 135 CE in an attempt to remove traces of Christianity. St Helena persuaded Constantine to build two churches on the site. They were begun in 326 and finished in 335. One of these was a domed building that housed a tomb cut out of the rock; the other covered the traditional site of Calvary, where Jesus was crucified. (Calvary is the Latin translation of Golgotha; see Matthew 27:33.) The site of Calvary was thought to be very close to the tomb because Jesus was crucified outside the city walls, and the tombs were also outside. Jesus was buried in a rich man's tomb, and this would have been near the city gates, near the place of execution. Helena's churches were destroyed by invaders and then rebuilt by the Crusaders, but all under one roof. (Look back at page 23 for a picture of the church today.)

It is now under the control of six Churches. The Greek Orthodox have the most influence, and the others are the Roman Catholics, the Armenians, the Syrians, the Copts and the Ethiopians.

▲ These pilgrims are praying at the tomb in the Church of the Holy Sepulchre.

a What is supposed to have happened here?
b What might these pilgrims be feeling?
c What would this place have looked like, originally?

At the place where Jesus was crucified, there was a garden, and in the garden a new tomb, in which no-one had ever been laid.

John 19:41

ROME

The city of Rome contains a small area called **Vatican** City, the headquarters of the Roman Catholic Church. Its huge, domed **St Peter's** rests upon the foundations of a much older church built by Emperor Constantine in the fourth century. Constantine believed that St Peter was buried beneath his church. Vatican hill had been a cemetery in earlier Roman times, and tradition held that Peter had been crucified in the reign of Emperor Nero and buried there by the early Christians.

There is a legend that Peter was fleeing from Rome during the first great persecution of Christians, when he met Jesus walking towards the city. Peter asked, '*Domine, quo vadis?*' ('Lord, where are you going?'), and Jesus answered, 'I go

▲ St Peter's Church, Rome.

to be crucified again.' Peter felt ashamed after seeing this vision, and returned to Rome where, on his insistence, he was crucified upside down because ordinary crucifixion was too good for him, as that had been done to his master. (There is a little church called *Domine Quo Vadis?* on the supposed spot.)

A New Approach – Christianity

St Paul is also said to have been killed at Rome during Nero's persecution in about 64 CE. As a Roman citizen he would have been beheaded outside the city wall. The traditional site was at the third milestone along the Laurentian Way, by the Salvian Marsh. A monastery was founded there in the seventh century. His body is thought to have been buried nearer to Rome, under the Church of St Paul-without-the-walls.

Rome is also an important pilgrimage site because that is where the Pope lives. Roman Catholics believe he is Peter's successor as head of the Church (see Matthew 16:18–19).

LOURDES

Lourdes, in the south of France, is a very popular place of pilgrimage. This is where St Bernadette is said to have seen the Virgin Mary. On Thursday 11 February 1858, when she was 14, Bernadette was out walking by a grotto. She heard what sounded like a gust of wind, but the trees did not move. Then she heard it again, and noticed that the branches of a rose bush in front of the entrance to the grotto were moving. By this was a gentle light that contained the figure of a beautiful woman, dressed in white, and she was smiling. Bernadette tried to move but could not at first. She made the sign of the cross, and stared at the woman. Then she felt at peace. She knelt down and said her rosary. The woman said hers, too, and then vanished.

The apparition appeared several more times, and when word got around many other people came to watch. They saw nothing, only Bernadette smiling, looking up as if in a trance. Eventually, the figure told Bernadette that she was the Virgin Mary and that a spring that

▲ St Bernadette.

▲ Our Lady of Lourdes.

appeared near her was to be visited by people who sought healing. Thousands of pilgrims now go to the spot, which today has a huge church and chapel built over it.

Since Lourdes became a centre of pilgrimage in the nineteenth century, there have been over 64 cases that have been declared as miraculous cures. If a person reports a cure, he or she is examined by a medical team at Lourdes, and the team will refer to the patient's home medical reports and doctor. The person will only be pronounced as cured if the complaint has totally disappeared and if there was no chance of the problem gradually getting better on its own or with normal medical treatment.

Many people, however, say they have felt much better after going there, though they are not completely cured. Others also say that the experience has helped them spiritually or emotionally, even though their physical illness has remained unchanged. One woman was afraid of losing her eyesight. She went to Lourdes and returned full of life and self-confidence, although her eyes had not improved. She felt she had been given the strength to cope with her problem.

SANTIAGO DE COMPOSTELA

The shrine of Santiago (St James) of Compostela was one of the most popular places of pilgrimage in the Middle Ages, ranking with Rome and the Holy Land. It is still a popular site for Roman Catholics.

Compostela lies in north-western Spain. A

▲ The pilgrims gather at night, holding candles. They walk around the shrine, singing praises to God.

The pilgrims above are at Lourdes.

a What happened at this place to turn it into a shrine?
b Why do many people come here?
c What happens if someone claims to have been healed?
d Can you think of an example of a healing said to have taken place at this shrine?
e What is the attraction of this place of pilgrimage?
f Imagine that you are a pilgrim at Lourdes. Write a letter home saying how you feel better as a result of prayer. You are not totally cured, though. How do you feel about this?

A New Approach – Christianity

local bishop ordered a site to be explored and excavated early in the ninth century when reports came to him of visions granted to an old hermit and to local peasants. The hermit had a dream in which he was told that the tomb of St James, the brother of St John, and son of Zebedee, and one of the twelve apostles, was in a wood near his home. The peasants reported seeing a star above the wood, and hearing heavenly music. An old Roman grave was found, and the bones were declared to be those of St James.

James was executed in about 44 CE in Jerusalem (see Acts 12:1–2). An eighth-century legend said he had preached in Spain after the resurrection, and that after his death his body had been taken there for safety. The presence of his tomb was even said to have converted a princess who built a shrine over it. This was forgotten about and it became surrounded by the wood.

A stone church was built over the shrine in the reign of Alfonso II (864–910) and it soon became a popular place of pilgrimage, whatever the truth behind the various legends. Spain needed a shrine and a patron saint at this time, as they were fighting the Muslim Moors for control of the land, and the idea of St James of Compostela rallied them and gave them hope.

Compostela became a place of international pilgrimage when Benedictine monks set up a community there after the defeat of the Muslims. Many came by sea, or by land through France ('The Way of St James'). There were many stories of miracles, such as one about an innocent boy who was framed for stealing a gold cup and was hanged. He was found alive on the gallows because St James was holding him up!

WALSINGHAM

Walsingham in Norfolk is known as 'England's Nazareth' because it is said that in the Middle Ages a replica of the Virgin Mary's home in Nazareth was built there. In 1061, the Lady of the Manor, Richeldis de Faverches, had a vision of the Virgin's home in Nazareth, and was instructed to build a copy nearby. Various legends surround the story of the building of the original shrine. One says that the builders had

▲ **Our Lady of Walsingham.**

numerous problems in constructing the shrine. Then one day they found that it had moved 200 yards away and miraculously built itself. Augustinian brothers became the guardians of the shrine in about 1169. It became popular because the way to the Holy Land was blocked by Muslim conquests, and so 'England's Nazareth' was visited instead. There were two attractions: a statue of Our Lady of Walsingham, and a phial said to contain milk from Mary's breasts. (There were many such relics around at the time and a learned man of the day, Erasmus, said that the phial probably contained a chalk mixture instead!)

The pilgrims would remove their shoes to walk the last mile to the shrine at the Slipper Chapel at Houghton St Giles (which is now a Roman Catholic church). The Red Mount Chapel was built to house pilgrims at King's Lynn in 1485, and the shrine seems to have been at the height of its popularity in the fifteenth century. It was destroyed by a Protestant mob in Henry VIII's reign, when many shrines and monasteries were demolished in order to seize their money and stop any influence by the Pope in England. The statue of Our Lady was taken to Smithfield in London and burnt.

The story of the renewal of the shrine begins when the Rev. A. Hope Patten became vicar of

Little Walsingham parish church in 1921. He had a copy of the statue made from an image on the seal that had survived and he placed it in the parish church. A copy of the shrine was built ten years later, and the statue was placed there. Crowds of pilgrims have flocked there ever since. The Orthodox have a small chapel with the Anglican Shrine Church. The Roman Catholics have converted the old Slipper Chapel into a shrine. Many Christians who go there say they find the experience restful and that it is spiritually refreshing to have a few days away from the normal pace of life. There were many stories of healings in the Middle Ages and there are still some claims made today. Thanksgiving plaques are placed in the wall for answered prayers.

CANTERBURY

St Thomas Becket, Archbishop of Canterbury, was murdered by four knights in Canterbury Cathedral on 29 December 1170. He was declared to be a saint only three years later because of his deeds of charity and the stories of miracles performed by asking for his prayers, or drinking water from St Mary's well into which his blood was said to have flowed. There were stories of the blind receiving their sight, of the lame walking and of a drowned boy being restored to life.

This saint became so popular that King Henry II, who had been responsible for his murder, performed a penance by walking bare-chested and barefoot through the streets of Canterbury to the cathedral. Monks whipped him along the way as he went to pray for forgiveness.

Pilgrims' ways were established, people travelling via Portsmouth, Southampton, Sandwich or

TASK BOX

a Which part of the shrine at Walsingham is shown here?
b What was supposed to have happened in the past?
c When and why was the first shrine destroyed?
d When was the new Anglican shrine built and what did the Roman Catholic shrine used to be?
e What do you think attracts people to this place of pilgrimage?
f Write out a thanksgiving plaque for someone who feels that they have been healed there.

A New Approach – Christianity

Winchester. Chaucer's pilgrims in *The Canterbury Tales* (written in the fourteenth century) went along the old Roman road, Watling Street, via London.

A Pilgrim's Hall was set up at Aylesford near Canterbury. A religious order has recently been established there again, and the hostel has been restored. Besides Henry II, Kings Richard I, Henry VIII and Louis VII of France visited Becket's tomb in the cathedral, and about 100,000 pilgrims visited the tomb in 1420, a sizeable proportion of the population.

Becket's tomb was so popular because he was a symbol of resistance against tyranny – against rulers who did not have the interests of the common people at heart. Henry VIII was particularly eager to destroy this shrine after his break with the Pope. Twenty-six wagons of gold and jewels were taken from it to fill Henry's treasury.

▲ The steps to Becket's tomb in Canterbury Cathedral.

> Jesus said, 'For whoever wants to save his life will lose it, but whoever loses his life for me will find it.'
>
> *Matthew 16:25*

PERSPECTIVES

In Christian language, however, our human journey is known as a pilgrimage; and a pilgrimage by definition, is never aimless and never solitary, either. We undertake it with serious intent, after thought and prayer. We have companions who don't merely travel beside us but often enrich our whole understanding of the way we are treading and of the object of our journey. And there goes with us, or before us, that unseen Companion who leads and preserves our steps, often when we think of him least, Jesus Christ, the way, the truth and the life.
Rt Rev Patrick Rodger

What does the bishop say that pilgrimage is all about?

LINDISFARNE (HOLY ISLAND)

This island is a few hundred yards off the Northumbrian coast, 60 miles north of Newcastle. At high tide, the island is cut off from the mainland for about five hours. It is about a mile and a half long, and a mile wide. It has a population of about 200, most of whom earn their living from fishing and tourism.

St Aidan came there with a group of monks in 634 at the request of King Oswald of Northumbria. He wanted Christianity to spread in his kingdom, so he gave the monks a base to work from. The monks lived in simple huts, and a large monastery was built there in the Middle Ages, which was closed by Henry VIII. It is now in ruins, but pilgrims meet there to hold services or to visit the small island church.

IONA

This is an island about a mile off the coast of West Scotland. It is three miles long and about a mile and a half wide. St Columba came there in 563 with a group of monks. They lived in simple huts and visited the mainland to teach the people about Jesus. They converted some of the Saxon kings, some of whom were buried on Iona. The island was regarded as a holy place. A larger monastery was built on the island in the Middle Ages, but this was closed by Henry VIII. The island was owned by the Dukes of Argyll until the eighth Duke gave it to the Church of Scotland in 1899.

The island became a centre of pilgrimage again in the 1930s. A minister in a church near Glasgow, George Macleod, came there in 1938 with a group of young ministers and craftsmen. They stayed for a time, and then returned to the mainland to live ordinary lives. Other people came, sharing their lives together, and then returned home later. The process of coming and going has carried on since. The idea was to mix ordinary working people and church ministers together so that they could learn how to understand each other better. Many young people go to summer camps on the island every year to pray, discuss issues, and work.

The ruined monastery has been largely restored and members of any Church are free to hold services there.

TEST YOURSELF

1 Which apostle is Santiago de Compostela linked with?
2 Why is Iona special, and when was this rebuilt as a pilgrimage centre?
3 Why is Lindisfarne special?

TASK BOX

Design a brochure for one of the places of pilgrimage besides Lourdes and Walsingham. Make sure you include information about why this is a place of special pilgrimage. What do people do there? What do they seek?

KEY QUESTION

Evangelical Christians do not usually go on pilgrimages. What gatherings might they attend instead?

SPRING HARVEST

Evangelical Christians enjoy travelling to special praise or Bible weeks. These use showgrounds and holiday camps, which church groups take over. One of the most popular is 'Spring Harvest', which uses several Butlins Holiday Camps around Britain at Easter. There are speakers, huge praise meetings with modern instruments, and fun activities. People try to learn something new about God, or find what their next step should be in their faith journey.

A New Approach – Christianity

THE GREENBELT FESTIVAL

The Greenbelt Festival runs on August bank holiday weekend, and encourages the Arts. It is like a smaller-scale, Christian Glastonbury festival. This is a more youthful event than weeks such as 'Spring Harvest', with a main stage in the evenings presenting Christian and secular bands who use contemporary styles (rock, dance, techno, etc.), such as The World Wide Message Tribe. There are fashion shows, circus tents, an art gallery and a full film programme as well as worship times, Bible studies, and speakers who explore what it means to believe in God today.

Though this festival was started by evangelical Christians, it is popular with many different denominations and styles. There are Anglican monks and nuns present, and a Roman Catholic mass is held on site.

REMEMBER

- Pilgrims travel to special, holy places.
- Some places are holy because they are linked with an apostle or the life of Jesus.
- Some are special because of a vision of Mary.
- Some are special because they are linked with one of the saints.
- All these places can feel holy because they have been prayed in for generations.

TEST YOURSELF

A B C

1 What happens at Spring Harvest?
2 How is Greenbelt different?
3 Which festival is more ecumenical?

The following sites will cover Bethlehem, Lourdes, Walsingham, Iona, Greenbelt and Spring Harvest:

- www.pef.org.uk/ Bethlehem%20Pages/ EC529on.htm

- www.theturf.demon.co.uk/ lourdes.htm

- www.walsingham.org.uk

- www.iona.org.uk

- www.greenbelt.org.uk

- www.springharvest.co.uk

WEBLINKS

TASK BOX

a Design a poster for Greenbelt or Spring Harvest. What happens there and what would attract certain people?

b Use a meditation exercise to imagine going on a rewarding journey:

- Still yourself, counting breaths.
- Imagine that you are on a journey. Where are you? How are you travelling? Are you alone?
- You face some difficulties. What are these? How do you overcome them?
- You get to your destination and find something very special. What is it?
- Count ten breaths and then open your eyes.

1 Describe one place of pilgrimage. [8]

2 Explain why people think making a pilgrimage is important. [7]

3 'It's a waste of time travelling halfway around the world when God is with you everywhere!'
Do you agree? Give reasons for your answer, showing that you have considered other points of view. Refer to Christianity in your answer. [5]

4 What is a pilgrimage? [2]

5 Describe a centre of pilgrimage in the UK and say why it is special. [4]

6 Explain which places of pilgrimage have a connection with the life of Jesus. [4]

7 'Life is like a pilgrimage.'
Do you agree? Give reasons for your point of view and show consideration of the views of others. Refer to Christian beliefs in your answer. [5]

Assignment

A New Approach – Christianity

Glossary

Abba – Aramaic word for 'Father'

abortion – the termination of a pregnancy

Adam – Hebrew word for a human being

Advent – from the Latin 'arrival'. The four Sundays before Christmas

agape – Greek word for 'love' meaning costly, suffering love

alb – long white robe worn by Christian priests

altar – the holy table upon which the bread and wine are blessed

annulment – where a marriage is declared never to have properly taken place

apocalyptic – a style of writing that uses vivid symbols and poetry to describe the end of the world

Apocrypha – a collection of books that was included in the Greek translation of the Old Testament

apostolic – based upon the teaching of the apostles

Ascension – Jesus' return to heaven

Assumption – the belief that Mary was taken into heaven, body and soul

atonement – making peace, making up for doing something wrong

baptism – a ceremony of pouring water over a person, or being immersed in a pool of water. This symbolises dying to an old life, rising to a new one, and spiritual cleansing for the soul

baptistry – a small pool in a Baptist Church

Beatitudes – 'happy sayings'. A list of nine sayings of Jesus about lifestyles

Bible – from a Greek word meaning 'the books'

bishop – an overseer in the Church

Blessed Sacrament – some of the blessed communion bread reserved after the service is over

canon – a standard or rule. The canon of the Bible is the list of books it contains

canonisation – the process of making someone a saint in the Roman Catholic Church

cantor – a person who leads the singing in an Orthodox church

cardinal – a senior Roman Catholic Bishop

cathedral – a large church where the bishop is based

catholic – worldwide

chancel – the area of some churches where the choir sits

charismatic – a believer open to the renewal of the Holy Spirit

chasuble – a colourful poncho-style robe worn by priests at the eucharist

Christ – the Greek word for Messiah, or Anointed One

Christmas – 'the mass of Christ', celebrating the birth of Jesus

church – an assembly of Christian worshippers

committal – when a coffin is lowered into a grave, or the curtain closes at the crematorium. This is a final handing over to God

confession – owning up to what we have done wrong

consent – the part of the marriage service where the couple are asked if it is their intention that the vows are to be exchanged

conservative – people who seek to be careful, conserving, conserving tradition. They have a strong belief in the Scriptures but are open to question certain things

contemplation – silent prayer and reflection; a form of meditation

consubstantiation – Luther's belief that the substance of bread and wine remained, joined to the substance of the body and blood of Christ

Counter-Reformation – a Roman Catholic movement that sought to reform the Church without becoming Protestant

creed – from 'Latin *credo*, 'I believe' A list of beliefs

deacon – Greek for 'server'

demi-gods – half-human, half-god figures in Greek and Roman myths

denomination – one type of church, or group of believers

diocese – a group of churches under a bishop

Easter – the celebration of the resurrection of Jesus

ecumenism – the churches working together for unity

ekklesia – the Assembly, or Gathering – the Greek word for 'church'

elder – an early name for a church leader, later called a 'priest'

encolpion – medallion worn by an Orthodox bishop with a picture of Mary on it

Epiphany – 'the appearance' of Jesus to the magi or wise men

episkopos – Greek for 'overseer' or bishop

epistle – a letter

eternal – something that lasts forever

eucharist – Greek for 'thanksgiving'. A thanksgiving meal using bread and wine, or Holy Communion

excommunicated – not allowed to receive Holy Communion

font – the place where people are baptised

fundamentalist – someone who believes that everything in the Bible should be taken as the absolute Word of God

Gehenna – a valley outside Jerusalem where rubbish was burnt Jesus used this as an image for judgement

genuflection – going down on one knee to show respect for the Blessed Sacrament

God the Son – the Second Person of the Trinity

Good Friday – the day recalls Jesus' dying on the cross

Gospel – a 'good news' book about the life of Jesus

grace – undeserved favour from God

Ground of our Being – a term for God that tries to express his vastness, depth and mystery

heresy – splitting away from the Church and holding unorthodox teaching

Holy Communion – sharing bread and wine to remember the death and resurrection of Jesus

Holy Sepulchre – the site believed to be the tomb where Jesus' body lay

Holy Trinity – God as Father, Son and Holy Spirit

Holy Week – remembering the last week of Jesus' life

ichthus – Greek for 'fish' and an early Christian code word, standing for 'Jesus Christ, Son of God, Saviour'

iconostasis – a screen covered with icons in front of an Orthodox altar

incarnation – the idea that God became a human being in Jesus

incense – scented tree gum burnt in worship

infinite – something that has no ending

inquisition – a movement that sought to stamp out heresy in the medieval Roman Catholic Church

Jesus Prayer – Orthodox prayer, 'Lord Jesus Christ, Son of God, have mercy on us'

Lent – the five weeks before Easter. A period of fasting and preparation

lectern – the stand where the Bible is kept

Liberation Theology – a movement that seeks to apply Christian teaching to society and to champion the cause of the poor

liberal – someone who is much freer in his or her interpretation of the Bible, questioning many things

magi – the wise men, from 'magus', meaning wise person, usually a magician or stargazer

Maundy Thursday – the day on which Jesus' washing of his disciples feet and sharing of the Last Supper is commemorated

mortal sin – sin that is serious and deadly to the soul

narthex – the entrance hall of an Orthodox church

original sin – a condition stemming from the disobedience of Adam and Eve, though there are different understandings of what has been passed down

Palm Sunday – the day that Jesus' entry into Jerusalem on a donkey is remembered

paraclete – a helper, counsellor or advocate; a name for the Holy Spirit

Parousia – the return of Christ at the end of time

Passion – the story of Jesus' journey to the cross

peace – a handshake, kiss or an embrace to show that believers all belong to one spiritual family

Pentecost – the time when the gift of the Holy Spirit was given to the disciples

pilgrimage – travelling to a holy place to pray and worship

Pope – the Bishop of Rome

prayer rope – Orthodox Christian rope with many knots. The Jesus Prayer is said on these

presbyter – Greek for 'elder' or priest

prophecy – a word from God for the present or the future

protestant – a protestor against the power of the Pope

pulpit – a raised platform where the sermon is traditionally preached from

purgatory – Roman Catholic belief in a place of preparation for heaven for those who are saved

reconciliation – making peace between two parties; also a sacrament where a person confesses before a priest

registrar – a person authorised to perform a marriage and sign the register

Reformation – a movement that sought to change the medieval Church

repentance – 'turning' from sin and wrong ways

rosary – a Roman Catholic set of prayer beads with which the Hail Mary prayer is recited

Royal Doors – the doors leading to the altar in the iconostasis

St Peter's basilica – the main church in the Vatican

sacrament – an action that conveys a spiritual blessing

sacrifice – an offering of time and effort

saint – 'one set apart', the name for any believer in the New Testament but often used of an especially holy believer

salvation – mending a broken relationship, setting free, acceptance and healing

Saturnalia – the pagan Roman New Year festival on 25 December

sermon – the preaching or address by the minister in a church service

servant – a mysterious figure in the Hebrew Bible who will suffer and die for the sins of humanity

sin – 'missing the mark'; falling short of what is right

sistrum – an Ethiopian Christian rattle

Son of God – a term with many meanings such as 'holy person', the King, or, of Jesus, the Second Person of the Trinity

spirit – something invisible In human terms, values and feelings Of God, his invisible nature that can be everywhere at once

stefana – the crowns used in an Orthodox marriage service

stole – colourful scarf worn by Christian priests

stoup – small container for holy water by a church door

structural sin – inherited wrong in systems and social structures that keep injustice going

supplication – a prayer asking for help from God

surplice – a long, white robe used by some clergy

testament – a binding promise. The Old Testament contained the Law and the promise that God would be with Israel. The New Testament contains the promise that God forgives and accepts us through Jesus' death on the cross

Torah – the Law of Moses found in the first five books of the Old Testament

transignification – a modern idea among some Roman Catholics to explain how bread and wine become the body and blood. They change their significance in the minds of the worshippers

transubstantiation – the traditional Roman Catholic view that the substance of bread and wine changes into that of the body and blood of Christ

The Vatican – the area of Rome where the Pope lives

venial sin – less serious sin that is not so hurtful

vigil – a late-night service of preparation

Virgin Birth – the belief that Jesus was conceived in the womb of a virgin, Mary

vocation – a personal calling to be a Christian minister or to live in a religious community as a monk or a nun

vows – special, sacred promises made by the bride and groom

Word – part of God acting in the world

Index

(page references to illustrations are indicated by *italic* type)

A New Approach – Christianity